First World War
and Army of Occupation
War Diary
France, Belgium and Germany

48 DIVISION
Headquarters, Branches and Services
Royal Army Veterinary Corps
Assistant Director Veterinary Services
3 April 1915 - 29 October 1917

WO95/2748/4

The Naval & Military Press Ltd
www.nmarchive.com
Published in association with The National Archives

Published by

The Naval & Military Press Ltd

Unit 10 Ridgewood Industrial Park,

Uckfield, East Sussex,

TN22 5QE England

Tel: +44 (0) 1825 749494

www.naval-military-press.com

www.nmarchive.com

This diary has been reprinted in facsimile from the original. Any imperfections are inevitably reproduced and the quality may fall short of modern type and cartographic standards.

© Crown Copyright
Images reproduced by permission of The National Archives, London, England, 2015.

Contents

Document type	Place/Title	Date From	Date To
Heading	WO95/2748 48 Div Apr 15-Oct 17 Ass Dir Vet Services		
Heading	48th Division A. Dir Veterinary Services Apr 1915-Oct 1917		
Heading	A.D.V.S South Midland Division Vol I 3-25.4.15		
War Diary		03/04/1915	25/04/1915
Heading	ADVS 48th Division Vol II 1-31.5.15		
War Diary	Nieppe	01/05/1915	31/05/1915
Heading	48th Division ADVS 48th Division Vol III 27-30.6.15		
War Diary	Nieppe	27/06/1915	30/06/1915
Heading	48th Division ADVS 48th Division Vol IV 1-31-7-15		
War Diary		01/07/1915	31/07/1915
Heading	48th Division ADVS 48th Division Vol V August 15		
War Diary		01/08/1915	31/08/1915
Heading	48th Division ADVS 48th Division Vol VI Sept 15		
War Diary		06/09/1915	30/09/1915
Heading	A.D.V.S 48div Oct 15 Vol VII		
War Diary		01/10/1915	31/10/1915
Heading	A.D.V.S 48th Div Nov Vol VIII		
War Diary	H.Q 48th Division	05/11/1915	30/11/1915
Heading	A.D.V.S 48th Div Dec Vol IX		
War Diary	H Qrs 48th Sm Div	09/12/1915	30/12/1915
Heading	A.D.V.S 48th Div Jan Vol X		
War Diary		01/01/1916	29/01/1916
Heading	A.D.V.S 48th Div Vol XI		
War Diary	Louvencourt	01/02/1916	02/02/1916
War Diary	Hd. Qrs	02/02/1916	29/02/1916
Heading	Advs 48th Div Vol XII		
War Diary	Headquarters	11/03/1916	31/03/1916
Heading	Advs 48th Div Vol XIII		
War Diary	Hd Qrs 48th Division	01/04/1916	18/05/1916
War Diary	Hd Qrs Army	18/05/1916	25/05/1916
War Diary	Hd Qr 48 Divn	30/05/1916	13/06/1916
War Diary	Hd Qr 48 Sm Divn	14/06/1916	30/06/1916
War Diary	HQ. Division	01/07/1916	10/07/1916
War Diary	HQ. 48th Divn	11/07/1916	17/07/1916
War Diary	HQ Division	18/07/1916	31/07/1916
War Diary	Headquarters Le Plouy	01/08/1916	08/08/1916
War Diary	Headquarters Beauval	09/08/1916	13/08/1916
War Diary	Headquarters Bouzincourt	13/08/1916	28/08/1916
War Diary	Headquarters Bertrancourt	29/08/1916	30/08/1916
War Diary	H.Q 48th Division	01/09/1916	20/09/1916
War Diary	H.Q Reserve Army	21/09/1916	30/09/1916
Miscellaneous	H.Q "Q" 48th Division	06/11/1916	06/11/1916
War Diary	H.Qrs Reserve Army	01/10/1916	08/10/1916
War Diary	H. Qrs 48th Div	09/10/1916	31/12/1916
War Diary	Headquarters 48th Division	01/01/1917	31/01/1917
War Diary	Headquarters 48th Division	01/02/1917	26/06/1917
War Diary	H.2 48th Div	27/06/1917	30/06/1917
War Diary	Beaulencourt P De C	01/07/1917	03/07/1917

War Diary	Bihucourt PLC Adinfer	04/07/1917	15/07/1917
War Diary	Adinfer P.d.C	16/07/1917	31/07/1917
War Diary	Hd Qrs 48th Div 18 Corps Area	01/08/1917	28/08/1917
War Diary	Wormhout	29/08/1917	18/09/1917
War Diary	Zutkerke	18/09/1917	27/09/1917
War Diary	Brake Camp	28/09/1917	30/09/1917
War Diary	C Camp N Poperinghe	01/10/1917	09/10/1917
War Diary	X Camp "C" Camp N Poperinghe	10/10/1917	12/10/1917
War Diary	Pernes	13/10/1917	16/10/1917
War Diary	Villers Chatel	17/10/1917	17/10/1917
War Diary	W30b53 (36B)	18/10/1917	29/10/1917

WO95/2748 (4)
48 Div
Apr '15 – Oct '17
Ass Dir Vet Services

48TH DIVISION

BEF

A. DIR. VETERINARY SERVICES
APR 1915 - ~~FEB 1919~~
OCT 1917

TO ITALY

A.D.V.S. South Midland Division

Vol I 3 — 25.4.15

Army Form C. 2118.

WAR DIARY
or
INTELLIGENCE SUMMARY.
(Erase heading not required.)

Instructions regarding War Diaries and Intelligence Summaries are contained in F.S. Regs., Part II. and the Staff Manual respectively. Title pages will be prepared in manuscript.

Hour, Date, Place	Summary of Events and Information	Remarks and references to Appendices
3rd April 1915.	South Midland Division Mobile Veterinary Section arrived at CASSEL — It is suggested that on a Division moving from home to this country, the Veterinary Section should move with advance units, at its work commences the moment Division units arrive at rail head —	
6th April 1915.	Section moved to La CRÈCHE conforming to further forward move of Division.	
25th April 1915	A memorandum received from D.V.S. G.H.Q. cancelling arrangements for payment of farmers by O.C. Mobile Veterinary Section, for the keep of sick horses left in their care. The procedure suggested in D.V.S. memo No 15/1353/15 in my opinion must hamper efficiency. The present system is a troublesome one, in that the Gables to hand at once on taking over the animal, and so terminating the contract	

Army Form C. 2118.

WAR DIARY
or
INTELLIGENCE SUMMARY.
(Erase heading not required.)

Instructions regarding War Diaries and Intelligence Summaries are contained in F.S. Regs., Part II. and the Staff Manual respectively. Title pages will be prepared in manuscript.

Hour, Date, Place	Summary of Events and Information	Remarks and references to Appendices
H.Q. S.M.D. 30.4.15.	I therefore strongly recommend a continuance of the previous procedure. The question of the supply of a float has been put forward & recommended by me. The money saved in horse flesh by the use of this commodity by a mobile veterinary section would be a considerable asset. All veterinary officers with whom I have conferred on the subject agree as to the value of a float for a mobile veterinary section. C.B.M Harris Lt. Col. A.D.V.S. S.M.D.	

ADVS. 48th Division

Vol II 1 — 31. 5. 15

WAR DIARY
or
INTELLIGENCE SUMMARY.
(Erase heading not required.)

Army Form C. 2118.

48th (SM) Division
VETERINARY

Hour, Date, Place	Summary of Events and Information	Remarks and references to Appendices
NIEPPE. 1st to 31st May 1915.	As the question of the supply of a small car for A.D.S of V.S of Division with so little authorized is not settled vide G.H.Q letter 983/14 dated 2.3.15. D.V.S. a speedy compliance is desirable. The want of such a commodity hampers one's work considerably. Take my own case — in addition to my administrative work with Divisional troops spread over a fairly wide area I have executive charge of 5 smaller units and it is next to impossible to carry out systematic — periodical inspections in the saddle, owing to the state of the roads and the distances — C.B.M Harris Lt Col A.D.V.S. 48th Division H.Q 48th(SM)Division 31-5-15	G.H.Q letter D.V.S No 983/14 dated 2.3.15.

ans.

107/5991

48th Division

A.D.V.S. 48th Division

Vol III 27—30. 6-15

WAR DIARY
or
INTELLIGENCE SUMMARY.

(Erase heading not required.)

VETERINARY Army Form C. 2118.
48th (S.M.) Division.

Hour, Date, Place	Summary of Events and Information	Remarks and references to Appendices
10. A.M. 27 June 1915. NIEPPE.	Headquarters of Division moved to BUSNES. 48th Mobile Veterinary Section moved with last group of Divison and halted at VIEUX BERQUIN - Ao & V.O's unsuccessfully accompanied the Troops. Efforts were made to obtain instructions for Veterinary Section to go forward to its base at MENSACQ near LILLERS —	
28th June 1915	Section halted at ROBECQ.	
29" June 1915	Arranged site for Section - Headquarters moved to CHATEAU PHILOMEL, near LILLERS. I was asked to remain at BUSNES —	
30. June 1915	Section moved into its billet at MENSACQ near LILLERS. I wish to suggest the advisability of a Mobile Veterinary Section receiving orders to move forward to its new destination with advance	

Army Form C. 2118.

(2)

WAR DIARY
or
INTELLIGENCE SUMMARY.
(Erase heading not required.)

Hour, Date, Place	Summary of Events and Information	Remarks and references to Appendices

units. In my opinion it should complete its work at its last station & move forward to start its quarantine at the earliest moment. There should be no difficulty as the personnel is a small one, it is very mobile, and can carry 3 days rations. Many would be saved by this procedure as sick horses left at Farms would be collected and the billeting expenses incurred considerably decreased. These conditions were represented during the time under report, but I failed to obtain sympathy appreciation.

C.Bm Harris Lt Col.
ADVS 48. (Sm) Division

HQ. 48ᵗʰ Sm Division
30 June 1915

48th Division.

121/6273

ADVS. 48th Division.

Vol IV

1-31-7-15

WAR DIARY or INTELLIGENCE SUMMARY

Army Form C. 2118.

VETERINARY — 48 (S.M.) DIVISION

Hour, Date, Place	Summary of Events and Information	Remarks and references to Appendices
1. July 1915. 6. July 1915.	Moved office from BISNES to LILLERS. To Advance Remount Depot, GONNEHEM to select Remounts for the Division.	
7th July 1915.	Arranged casting parade to A.D.R. 1st Army and with him to GONNEHEM (Advance Remount Depot) to select Remounts.	
10th July 1915.	Left for England on leave. Capt. Lewis Green, A.V.C. (T) /c 2nd Brigade, R.F.A. acting for me.	
17th July 1915.	Capt. Lewis Green, A.V.C. (T) under GONNEHEM and selected Remounts for the Division, prior to its move. Arrangements made for evacuation of all sick horses of Division prior to its move. Lt. Philipson, A.V.C. Comm'dg. Horse Rly. left for ENGLAND on leave. Returned from leave and joined Division at TERRESMENIL.	
18th July 1915.		
19 July 1915.	Arranged Cards for mobile veterinary section.	

WAR DIARY
or
INTELLIGENCE SUMMARY.
(Erase heading not required.)

Army Form C. 2118.

II

Hour, Date, Place	Summary of Events and Information	Remarks and references to Appendices
19th July 1915.	To DOULLENS to obtain Section and marched with it ?along to its new billets at TERRESMESNIL.	
20th July 1915.	Division continued its move. Marched Section to AUTHIE. Arranged billets for Section in the open. Much crowded with other units and unable to do its work.	
21st July 1915.	To Headquarters 3rd Army to report arrivals to D.D.V.S. - He had not arrived.	
22nd July 1915.	To SARTON to select site for M.V.S. Arranged all satisfactorily with Maire and Curé. Fixed with D.A. & ?M.L., 7th Corps, that Section takes take up its quarters in SARTON. This is a favour as SARTON has been declared out of our Division area.	
23rd to 31st July 1915	Division still taking up its positions and moving daily. It is impossible to maintain strict veterinary supervision under the circumstances, but things are straightening out eventually.	

CBMHams? Lt.Col.
A.D.V.S. 48th Division.

2/8/15.

121/6737

48th Division

A.D.V.S. 48th Division
Vol V
August 15

WAR DIARY or INTELLIGENCE SUMMARY

Army Form C. 2118.

VETERINARY.
48th (S.M.) Division

Hour, Date, Place	Summary of Events and Information	Remarks and references to Appendices
1915		
1 August	48th Mobile Veterinary Section moved to SARTON.	
16 August	Captain Lewis Green, A.V.C.(T) the senior Army Veterinary Officer ordered to report to War Office as A.D.V.S. on T.F. Division. This withdrawal now brings the strength of Veterinary Establishment down to reduced organization of a Division. My second charger has been withdrawn, and the motor car sanctioned for A.D.V.S. in War Office letter 17/1630 (V.D.) dated 2nd July last, has been withheld. It is impossible to carry on one's work efficiently under such circumstances. To there is no post of A.D.V.S. of a Division is unsatisfactory, as the Veterinary side is not one's such & sufficient importance to warrant a fair share of the [ ] so-called pool.	
23 August	Lieut. V. Price-Jones A.V.C.(T) commanding Mobile Veterinary Section returned from leave. On relief Capt. Farrell, A.V.C.T. posted to 48th Divisional Train vice Lieut. C.S. Thorn A.V.C.(T.C) appointed to 1st F.A. Brigade of Division. On the wheelers mentioned above 3 V.O.'s carry out the work of the 4 Brigades of the Divisional Artillery —	

WAR DIARY
or
INTELLIGENCE SUMMARY.
(Erase heading not required.)

Army Form C. 2118.

Instructions regarding War Diaries and Intelligence Summaries are contained in F.S. Regs., Part II and the Staff Manual respectively. Title pages will be prepared in manuscript.

Hour, Date, Place	Summary of Events and Information	Remarks and references to Appendices
1915 1st to 31st August	Put up suggestions during month for the "Ricking" of standings for horses for the coming winter, & for an improved system of watering horses in some units, & for the meeting of Remounts at Railhead — 40 horses of the Division have been ordered inefficient during the month in consequence of "picking up" nails — Suggestions put forward with a view to prevention — The Section is now understrength. (2 privates sick) Reinforcements have been demanded in the usual order, A.7.B.213 but have not yet arrived. Miles travelled during month 300. C.B.M.Morris Lt Col ADVS 48th Division 2nd Sept. 1915.	

12/7107

48th Division

A.D.V.S. 48th Division
Vol VI
Sept 15

Army Form C. 2118.

VETERINARY
48th (S.M.) Division

WAR DIARY
or
INTELLIGENCE SUMMARY.
(Erase heading not required.)

Hour, Date, Place	Summary of Events and Information	Remarks and references to Appendices
1915		
6th September to 30th September	Suspicious cases of Glanders reported in horses of 3rd Battery, 3rd (Berwick) Brigade R.A. – Post mortem examination made on destruction of these animals, and evidence of disease confirmed. With the assistance of Lieuts F.E. Heath, C.S. Keane, J.C. Grant, and W.F. Darling, 550 horses of the Brigade were tested with mallein, and 19 horses reacted to the test – These 19 animals were destroyed, post-mortem examinations made, and evidence of disease confirmed in all cases – Sanitary and other precautionary measures were adopted to stamp out the disease, and so far as it is possible to conclude, the Brigade now is free from the disease – Major Holiday QVC arrived on the 30th Sept. to carry out the intra-dermal palpebral test in the horses of the affected Battery and with negative results. The wastage of horses for the Division during the month reached the figure of 3.02% accounted for by an increased	

Army Form C. 21

WAR DIARY
or
INTELLIGENCE SUMMARY.
(Erase heading not required.)

Instructions regarding War Diaries and Intelligence Summaries are contained in F. S. Regs., Part II. and the Staff Manual respectively. Title pages will be prepared in manuscript.

Place	Date	Hour	Summary of Events and Information	Remarks and references to Appendices
	1915			
	6th September to 30th September		Number of horses evacuated, owing to possibility of a move and accidents resulting in injuries due to bad stable management. This latter condition is being dealt with by Headquarters of the Division.	
			Miles travelled during the month – 380.	

G.B.M. Harris Lt Col.
A.D.V.S. 48th Div.

121/7496

A.D.U.S. 48 An.

Oct. 15

Vol VII

Army Form C. 2118

WAR DIARY
or
INTELLIGENCE SUMMARY.

(Erase heading not required.)

VETERINARY
48th DIVISION.

Instructions regarding War Diaries and Intelligence Summaries are contained in F.S. Regs., Part II. and the Staff Manual respectively. Title pages will be prepared in manuscript.

Place	Date	Hour	Summary of Events and Information	Remarks and references to Appendices
	1st to 4th October 1915.		Completed testing for Glanders amongst horses of 3rd Warwick Brigade R.F.A. with the dermal-palpebral system demonstrated by Major Hobday a/c. No animal responded to the test revealing the fact that an previous work with the ordinary "Mallein" test had been thoroughly carried out.	
	5th to 31st October 1915.		Ordinary routine has occupied the remaining days of the month with nothing unusual to report. Horse management has improved in the units, so the result it is hoped of the steps taken by Headquarters Division to bring about this condition. Wass cage for the month 2.%. Mules Evacuated during the month 400.	

C. B. M. Harris Lt. Col.
A.D.V.S. 48th Division.

ADDIS. 48ù En
Nov
Vol VIII

12/7663

WAR DIARY or INTELLIGENCE SUMMARY

Army Form C.2118

VETERINARY
48th (S. M.) Division

Place	Date	Hour	Summary of Events and Information	Remarks and references to Appendices
H.Q. 48th Division	Nov 5		Detailed Lieut Darling AVC. ? ? a/c 1st Brigade. R.F.A. to proceed from D.Div. 3rd Army to proceed to H.Q. 27th Division to assist in Mallein testing horses of that Division	
"	8th		First appearance of Mange amongst horses of this Division on the 3rd Field Ambulance R.A.M.C. Microscopical examination revealed Complaint of Psoroptic type - Issued orders as stated in S.R.O. 441.	
"	11th		Mange appears amongst horses of "17" Brigade R.F.A. now attached to this Division - S.R.O 441 carried out. No 5 Serg.t Probert A.V.C. 7.7, the senior N.C.O of the mobile Reported. Serg.t Probert A.V.C. 7.7, the senior N.C.O of the mobile Veterinary Section for incompetency and asked authority to return him to England for duty under a senior N.C.O.	
"	16th		The Corps Army Commander ordered the reduction of Serg.t Probert and ruled that he was to continue to serve in his unit.	
"	20th		Put up a further request for Serg.t Probert pointing out that difficulties would arise if this NCO remained in his unit after retention	

Army Form C. 2118

WAR DIARY
or
INTELLIGENCE SUMMARY.
(Erase heading not required.)

Place	Date	Hour	Summary of Events and Information	Remarks and references to Appendices
HQ. 48th Division	Nov 20th		G.O.C. 48th Division reinstituting the case to Corps. Mange appears amongst horses of 48th Divisional Ammunition Column - Routine stead in G.R.O. 441 carried out.	
"	24		Inspected horses of 17th Brigade R.G.A. - Animals in very good condition, and Lieut. Coombs V.O. % working hard to prevent spread of Mange.	
"	25		Inspected Mange Cases and animals exposed to contact with Mange in 48th Divisional Ammunition Column — V.O. % Lieut. Prob. Jones. handling the situation effectively.	
"	30.		No 16. Sergt W. Thom Bray Ave. V.J. S.M. mobile V.G.y Section reported by O.C. Section for neglect of duty. Miles travelled during month 280	

C.B. M Harries Lt Col.
ADVS 48th Division

7/12/15.

A.D.v.S. hőgés Dr.
Dae
vol. IX

12/1957

A.D.u.S. 48ú D.
Dec.
vol. IX

12/7957

Army Form C. 2118.

WAR DIARY
or
INTELLIGENCE SUMMARY.
(Erase heading not required.)

VETERINARY.
48th S M DIVISION

Place	Date	Hour	Summary of Events and Information	Remarks and references to Appendices
HdQrs 48 S M Divn	9. Dec		Wire received from ADVS. 3rd army, advising unfitness of Lieut. F.E. HEATH AVC 177 for overseas service for 12 months – Staff of Strength of Division accordingly. Services of Lieut. G. GREEN. AVC applied for.	ADVS. 3rd Army Wire No AV/97 of 9-12-15.
"	10th		Horse Ambulance, the gift of "The Dumb Friends League" arrived at Section.	
"	15th		Clerk to ADVS. No.1347 Corporal J. ASHBEE left on 1 months leave of absence on his signing on for a further period of service.	
"	20th		Mallein received for testing all horses of the Division by the dermo-palpebral method.	S.I.S.C. 1337 authority
"	20th		Lieut. G. GREEN. AVC. started his arrival. Taken on Strength of Division and posted to 3rd (Warwick) Brigade. R.F.A. for duty –	17/5376 of 9.12.15
"	28th		Started testing by Palpebral method horses of Headquarters. Time occupied fully in carrying out this operation – Lieut. V. PRIDE-JONES. AVC. ff Commanding Mob. Vety. Section left on 8 days leave of absence.	
"	30th		REMARKS. In consequence of the inclement weather and the depth of mud surrounding horse-standings, coupled with chiefly cracked hole have been massed and a big evacuation not resulted, but in condition the general good health of the horses is maintained. A case of Glanders was reported on the 27. Decr in a

Army Form C. 2118.

II

WAR DIARY
or
INTELLIGENCE SUMMARY.
(Erase heading not required.)

Place	Date	Hour	Summary of Events and Information	Remarks and references to Appendices
	31-12-15		Horse belonging to "B" Squadron, King Edward's Horse (Divisional Cavalry) evacuated to No 5 Veterinary Hospital, in the ordinary way. The bulk of the Squadron is being carried out under the general scheme. Miles travelled. 300. CJW Harris Lt. Col. A. D. of V. S. 48th (S. M.) Division.	

A. D. V. S. + H. Dev
Jan
Vol X

Army Form C. 2118.

WAR DIARY
or
INTELLIGENCE SUMMARY.
(Erase heading not required.)

VETERINARY
48th (S.M.) DIVISION

Instructions regarding War Diaries and Intelligence Summaries are contained in F.S. Regs. Part II. and the Staff Manual respectively. Title pages will be prepared in manuscript.

Place	Date	Hour	Summary of Events and Information	Remarks and references to Appendices
1916				
Jany	1	—	Stocktaking	
Jany	25		Completed test for Glanders on Division horses and mules. Total 5717 horses and 310 mules.	
Jany	12 to 17		To SARTON to carry out test for Glanders on horses of 7th Corps at MARIEUX. Carried out test on horses of #1 S.M. Mobile Veterinary Section.	
Jany	25		Lieut. Gaunt A.V.C. one N.C.O. and 10 other ranks A.V.C. proceeded to trenches at FONQUEVILLERS to fire 5 rounds at a target in enemy's trenches by order of the G.O.C. 48th Division.	
Jany	26		Lieut Darling, A.V.C. one N.C.O. and 10 other ranks A.V.C. proceeded to trenches at FONQUEVILLERS to fire 5 rounds at a target in enemy's trenches by order of the G.O.C. 48th Division.	
Jany	29		To SARTON (M.V.S.Colin) to look at and examine by pr.C. mortem two cases of Glanders revealed by test - Glanders and G.K. in both cases. Miles travelled on duty during month = 330.	

1. February 1916

C.B.M. Harris Lt. Col.
A.D. of V.S. 48M/S. M. I.

48

A.D.V.S. 48 D.w
———————
Vol XI

Army Form C. 2118.

WAR DIARY
or
INTELLIGENCE SUMMARY.
(Erase heading not required.)

"VETERINARY"
48th (S.M.) Division

Place	Date	Hour	Summary of Events and Information	Remarks and references to Appendices
LOUVENCOURT	1.2.16	9.30am	Distributed 143 Remounts to Units of Division.	
LOUVENCOURT	2.2.16		To Divisional Train to search for lost veterinary chests for units of Division. Executive round, correspondence and routine at H.Q.s	
H.Q.s	"		Issued 4/10 Horse Smoke Helmets to Units of Division.	
H.Q.s	3.2.16		Conference of V.O.s at Headquarters. Advice received of policy of Capt. Sellino are temporarily m.	
			Capt. Pride-Jones on sick leave. Orders received for Lieut. Gaunt a/c to take command of Mobile Veterinary Section. To SARTON to pay men of Section.	
H.Q.s	5.2.16		To SARTON to inspect Section. To LOUVENCOURT in search of lost medicines. To inspect horses of "B" Squadron King Edward's Horse. Inspected R.E. horses at Headquarters.	
H.Q.s	7.2.16		Inspected horses 5th Sussex Regt. and horses of 144th Inf. Brigade. Capt. Sellino a/c arrived to take over my no arrival. Sent him on to H.Q. Harrison Brigade R.F.A.	
H.Q.s	9.2.16		Lieut. Gaunt a/c took over command of Mobile Vety. Section.	
	10.2.16		To Section. Correspondence, executive round and routine.	
	12.2.16		To Section. Leave granted for 8 days. Arranged with Capt. Farrell a/c to take over my duties during absence.	
H.Q.s	13.2.16		Proceeded on leave.	
	14.2.16		Correspondence and executive round. Distributed 141 Remounts at AUTHIE to units of Division	
	15.2.16		Correspondence and executive round.	
	16.2.16		Correspondence and executive round.	
	17.2.16		Do Do	
	18.2.16		Conference of V.O.s. Railhead changed to LARBRET.	
	19.2.16		Correspondence and executive round.	
	20.2.16		Do	
	21.2.16		Do	

Army Form C. 2118.

WAR DIARY
or
INTELLIGENCE SUMMARY.
(Erase heading not required.)

II

Place	Date	Hour	Summary of Events and Information	Remarks and references to Appendices
H.Q.2.	22/2/16		Routine. Received wire advising that Lt.Col. Harris (A.D.V.S.) leave has been extended to 13th March 1916 on medical certificate.	
H/e 6.20	23.2.16		Routine. Visited D.D.V.S. 3rd Army.	
"	24.2.16		Routine. Arranged with A.A. re mg. 6" warm. 6" R. Warwick Regt. and 5th Honrigs. Bde. R.F.A. that their horses went to relieve for Flanders. — J.O. SARTON inspected horses of 9th Royal Scots on what to Flanders	
"	25.2.16		Conference of V.Os. — Arranged with Capt. Sellers to carry out relief for Flanders of the horses of 6th Warwicks and 5th Honrigs. B.Bury.	
"	26.2.16		Routine. Arranged with A.D.V.S. 4th Division to allow such animals of 48th Div.D.S.P. to be evacuated at DOULLENS. as the distance to our new railhead is too great.	
"	28.2.16		Correspondence and routine. — Sent of sick returns —	
"	29.2.16		Correspondence and routine. —	

C.B.M.Harris Lt. Col
A.D.V.S.
to Off.g A.D.V.S. 48. s.m. Division

19.3.16.

48

ad V.S. 48 Div
—————
Vol XII

Army Form C. 2118.

VETERINARY
48° (Sm) Division.

(I)

WAR DIARY
or
INTELLIGENCE SUMMARY.
(Erase heading not required.)

Instructions regarding War Diaries and Intelligence Summaries are contained in F. S. Regs., Part II. and the Staff Manual respectively. Title pages will be prepared in manuscript.

Place	Date	Hour	Summary of Events and Information	Remarks and references to Appendices
Headquarters	March 11th		Capt V Pride Jones, A.V.C. T.F. reported his return from 8 weeks sick leave of absence.	
"	14.3.16		A.D.V.S. reported from 3 weeks leave on medical certificate	
"	15.3.16		To Sedan to inspect. Posted Captain Pride Jones to 1st (Gloster) F.a. Brigade. Entire reserved to move mobile Vety Section from SARTON to FEMECHON. Put up notices to C.R.A. suggesting better methods of stable management, with a view to improving this condition	
"	18.3.16		of the knees of 1.2nd (Worcester) Brigade, R.F.a.	
"	20.3.16		D.D.V.S. & D.D.R. 4th Army called - To SLEEGER to inspect knees of 3rd (Warwick) Brigade RFA	
"	21.3.16		To FEMECHON to select site to Sedan	
"	22.3.16		To Sedan at SARTON. The unit moved this day to FEMECHON - To TALMAS to with Capt Sellers A.V.C. to see him treat up in accordance with instructions received from D.V.S. 4th Army. Capt Sellers AVC attached IF Division strength for this day. Capt Farrell A.V.C. to 48° Divisional Train left on 8 days Quarry Leave.	
"	24/3/16		To SOUASTRE and AETAIE to inspect knees of 143rd Infantry Brigade transport	
"	26/3/16		Headquarters Division moved to COUIN	
"	27/3/16		Inspected "D" Battery horses 4° Brigade RFa Evacuated to sedan 24 debilitated	

Army Form C. 2118.

WAR DIARY
or
INTELLIGENCE SUMMARY.
(Erase heading not required.)

(2)

Place	Date	Hour	Summary of Events and Information	Remarks and references to Appendices
Halysanli	29/3/16		Horses in very poor condition.	
			To ROSSIGNOL with V.O. & Capt. Hearn A.V.C. to inspect horses	
			Horses in very good condition.	
	30/3/16		To FERMETON to Indian to dispose of surplus horses. Office fixed up at last	
			C.P.M. Hearn. O.6C	
			A.D.V.S. 48° (SM) Division
	2 April 1916			

aWS 48 D 10

Vol XIII

XLVIII

Army Form C. 2118.

WAR DIARY
or
INTELLIGENCE SUMMARY.
(Erase heading not required.)

VETERINARY
48th (S.M.) Division

Place	Date	Hour	Summary of Events and Information	Remarks and references to Appendices
At Q.20 48th Division	April 1	—	Exercise for horse. To COIGNEUX with V.O's to see horse of 1st S.M. Brigade. R.F.A. – D.D.V.S. & Army called.	I.
"	" 3		To Railhead BELLE EGLISE to meet 100 Remounts for the Division. Distributed to R.A. To BUS R.C. O.D.V.S. 31st Division to veterinary care of Amm" Col" horse at BELLE EGLISE	
"	" 4		To FEMECHON to see work of 1st S.M. Mobile Veterinary Section – To SARTON with Sub. Amm. Officer to settle claim of Madame Boulimbert. Contract Inspection of Farm where Section was located.	
"	" 5		To BAPENCOURT to see horse of 145th Infantry Brigade – To St LEGER to pick out horse for 5th inoculated by O.C. 4th Battery 4th S.M. Brigade R.F.A.	
"	" 6		To AUTHIE to select H.D. horse of D.A.C. For transfer to 32nd Division. To FEMECHON to see work of the Section.	
"	" 7		Conference of V.O's. To St LEGER to see horses of 45th Battery, 7th Brigade R.F.A. All in very good condition. To see debilitated horses of 3rd S.M. Brigade R.F.A. for transfer to M.V.S.	
"	" 8		To AUTHIE and St LEGER round horses of 3rd and 4th Brigades R.F.A.	
"	" 9		To Railhead CANDAS to meet and return 158 Remounts for Division. To AUTHIE later.	
"	" 10		To distribute same to units of Division. To FEMECHON to Section – D.D.V.S. called.	
"	" 11		To AUTHIE to Mo Ambce Remounts – a pouring wet day. D.D.V.S. called. Took him round horses of Divisional Train, and 1st S.M. Mobile Veterinary Section at FEMECHON – To St LEGER to see horse of 3rd Brigade and Div. Amm" Column.	
"	" 12			

Army Form C. 2118.

WAR DIARY
or
INTELLIGENCE SUMMARY.
(Erase heading not required)

Instructions regarding War Diaries and Intelligence Summaries are contained in F. S. Regs., Part II. and the Staff Manual respectively. Title pages will be prepared in manuscript.

Place	Date	Hour	Summary of Events and Information	Remarks and references to Appendices
H.Q. 48 Div	April 13		To AUTHIE to inspect 12 H.D. horses of D.A.C. for 18th Division, and distributed 35 H.D.	
"	14th		Horses from D.A.C. to units of Division.	
"	15th		Conference of V.O's. To G.O.C's Conference.	
"	16th		Round horses of units at COUIN - Windy and snowy day	
"	17th		To FEMECHON to see work of Section.	
"	"		To FEMECHON to inspect horses personnel and horses of Section. To SOUASTRE to see horses of 2nd Field Co. R.E. - All in good condition, with exception of 2 chargers of C.O.	
"	18th		To G.O.C's Conference.	
"	19th		To FEMECHON to see work of Section	
"	20		To Railhead CANDAS to disem. 81 horses for the Division. To AUTHIE to distribute same to units	
"	21st		Conference of V.O's. To AUTHIE to hand over 10 H.D. horses from D.A.C. to 14th Reserve Park A.S.C.	Mileage. Not including visit to L. of C. 219 Miles.
"	23.		To ABBEVILLE to see Hospitals on L.of C. Horses 5th, 17th & 22nd Veterinary Hospitals	
"	24		To FORGES les EAUX to see 7th & 8th Veterinary Hospitals Round Convalescent Horse Depot at GOURNAY	
"	25		To FEMECHON to see work of Section	
"	26		Round horses of 144th Inf. Brigade.	
"	27		To FEMECHON to show an attached Staff Officer the work of the Section - To Railhead CANDAS to detrain 239 Remounts - To AUTHIE later to detrain same to units.	
"	28			
"	29.			
"	30			

5/5/16.

C. Britannia Lt Col
A.D.V.S. 48 Div.

ADVS
VETERINARY
48th (S.M.) Division

WAR DIARY
or
INTELLIGENCE SUMMARY.

Army Form C. 2118.

WO/14

Place	Date	Hour	Summary of Events and Information	Remarks and references to Appendices
H.Q. 48 Div.	May 1st to 6th		Routine	
	7th		Wire from A.D.V.S. Fourth Army that 2 cases evacuated to Base had reacted to the Mallein test. Found these animals belonged to the 5th Battery, 4th Brigade R.F.A. Called at Battery lines and gave verbal instructions as to procedure. Wrote C.R.A with regard to "D" Battery, 3rd Brigade.	
"	8th		To COIGNEUX to inspect H.Q. horses of 1st Brigade R.F.A. 8 Sergeants arrived from Depôt Leamington. 5 posted to 1st Brigade, and 3 to 4th Brigade R.F.A. To BEAUVAL, GEZAINCOURT and HEM to arrange veterinary care of units proceeding to that area.	
"	9th		To ST LEGER to inspect H.Q. horses of 3rd Brigade R.F.A. To Conference of ADVS. Fourth Army at Headquarters, QUERRIEUX.	
"	10th		"B" Squadron H.E.H. Left Division. Inspected H.Q. horses of 2nd Brigade R.F.A. at AUTHIE. So see horses to be left in 5th Battery, 4th Brigade with Capt. Darling are in V.O. in charge. To FIENVILLERS to see Mobile Veterinary Section. Wrote and posted small despatch on Glanders outbreak.	
"	11th		To inspect H.Q. horses of 4th Brigade R.F.A. To HEM to see V.O. in charge of troops in that area.	
"	12th		Conference of V.O's. To inspect Brigade Transport horses of 144th Infantry Brigade	

Army Form C. 2118.

WAR DIARY
or
INTELLIGENCE SUMMARY.
(Erase heading not required.)

Instructions regarding War Diaries and Intelligence Summaries are contained in F.S. Regs., Part II. and the Staff Manual respectively. Title pages will be prepared in manuscript.

Place	Date	Hour	Summary of Events and Information	Remarks and references to Appendices
H.Qrs 48 Div.	May 12th		To FEMECHON to see horse of 6th Battery, 4th Brigade, which had been given an unsatisfactory mallein test.	
"	13th		Sent in report on Glanders outbreak.	
"	14th		To inspect H.D. horses of Ammunition Column 2nd Brigade. - To BEAUVAL & HEM to see horses of 144th Infantry Brigade.	
"	15th		To meet D.D.V.S. Fourth Army at FEMECHON on Remount Cooling parade. To Annexe Column 1st and 2nd Brigades R.F.A. to select H.D. horses for transfer.	
"	16th		D.D.V.S. Fourth Army came to eat me to do two weeks stable & on leave.	
"	17th		To FEMECHON to see mules of 48th Divisional Train. To Section later.	
"	18th		To Headquarters Fourth Army to take over work of D.D.V.S.	
H.Qrs Army	18th to 30th		At Army Headquarters -	
H.Qrs 48 Div	25th		To HEM to inspect horse of 2nd Field Co. R.E. -	
" "	30th		Returned to Divisional Headquarters. Walked round horse of H.Q. units	
" "	31st		Settled up correspondence in my own office. To Divisional Ammunition Column and Mobile Veterinary Section in afternoon.	

C.B.M. Harris
Lt. Col.
A.D. of V.S. 48th (S.M.) Division.

WAR DIARY or INTELLIGENCE SUMMARY

Army Form C. 2118.

VETERINARY A.D.V.S. 48th (S.M.) Division I

TOC 15

Place	Date	Hour	Summary of Events and Information	Remarks and references to Appendices
H.Q. 48th Division	June 1	-	To Raihad (CANDAS) to meet 29 Remounts and stabled them to units later, at AUTHIE. Mobile Section at FAMECHON	
"	2		Conference of M.O's. Corporal Ashbee (Clerk) went on 8 days leave.	
"	3		To see 1st Brigade horses at COIGNEUX with M.O. To Section at FAMECHON.	
"	5		To No 29 Casualty Clearing Hospital to see Capt Farrell A.V.C. (To Training Area BEAUVAL + HEM) who had gone sick. To Section to see surplus horses.	
"	6		Outbreak of Mange amongst horses of 240" Brigade. R.F.A. Paraded dismounted 2 Mobile Battery horses and went round lines with Brigade Commander. To Section horses examined. Mange Cases and Cleans of Clanders 1 S. Battery. 4th Brigade horses. To ONEUX, AUGENVILLERS, to see horses of 145th Infantry Brigade. Capt Farrell GOC returned from Training area to FAMECHON.	
"	7			
"	8		To FAMECHON & held P.M. examination on leading horse of 4th Brigade. Des Brigade 2 horses affected with Glanders. To see horses of 3rd Field Ambulance at AUTHIE.	
"	10		To FAMECHON & made P.M. Examination of 3 horses which rocked – found Glanders. To AUTHIE. Saw horses in D.A.C.	
"	11		To Raihad (CANDAS) to meet 90 horses to units at AUTHIE.	
"	12		To COIGNEUX to see Mange Cases in 240 Brigade R.F.A. To Section in afternoon.	
"	13		Corporal Ashbee (Clerk) returned from leave. Promoted Private Wood to Corporal in Section. Sent P.M. Instruments to 31st Division. To Section at FAMECHON.	

Army Form C. 2118.

WAR DIARY
or
INTELLIGENCE SUMMARY.
(Erase heading not required.)

II

Place	Date	Hour	Summary of Events and Information	Remarks and references to Appendices
HdQrs 48th S.M.	June 14		Capt. V. Poke Jones returned from leave. To see horses of 145th 2nd Bde. Transport with V.O's (Capt Heam) Draper.	
	" 15		To COIGNEUX to arrange site for Advanced Collecting Station with 2nd A.M.B. To Conference at H.Q.	
	" 16		Conference of V.O's. Splinted work during fighting. To FAMECHON to inspect horses Remounts.	
	" 17		To COIGNEUX to see horses of DAC and horses of 2nd & Brigade R.F.A. To 145 Inf Bde Transport Lines.	
	" 18		To COIGNEUX with Capt Gould A.V.C. examd Selectn. 1 R.CO + 2 men to rehearse sorts for withdrawal of casualties from front line. To Army HQ for DDVS' Conference.	
	" 19		To COIGNEUX to fix up Advanced Section. To FAMECHON to see cases for evacuation	
	" 20		To FAMECHON on casting parade of D.A.R. 4th Army. To Railhead BELLE EGLISE to meet 133 Remounts and to AUTHIE water to distribute to units.	
	" 21		To Advanced Section at COIGNEUX and M.V.S. at FAMECHON.	
	" 22		Do. Do. Do. Inspected on horse of 48th Divl. Train.	
	" 24		"A" day. Round horses of trsp of Lancashire Hussars. Walk to A mount to M.V.S. at FAMECHON	
	" 25		B. day. To Railhead to meet 14 Remounts. To FAMECHON afternoon to disable. Round Hotchkiss Sect Lancashire Hussars. To Advanced Rly Schon and M.V. Sectn.	
	" 26		Capt Heam AVC returned from leave.	
	" 27		To see horses of Machine Gun Sectn Lancashire Hussars. To FAMECHON to Selectn	
	" 28		D. day. Postponement of gardens F.f. 48 hours.	
	" 29		To FAMECHON to Selectn	
	" 30		Orders to advance M.V.S. from FAMECHON to COIGNEUX. made arrangements	

C.B.M. Harris
Lt. Col.
7/7/16
A. D. of V. S. 48th (S. M.) Division.

VETERINARY. Army Form C. 2118.
48th (S.M.) DIVISION

VOL 16

WAR DIARY
or
INTELLIGENCE SUMMARY.
(Erase heading not required.)

Place	Date	Hour	Summary of Events and Information	Remarks and references to Appendices
1916 July H.Q. Division	1916 July 1.		To meet Mobile Vet Section at FAMECHON and lead to Bivouacs on the ST LEGER-COISNEUX road (J 74). To Advanced Section in afternoon	
"	" 2.		To Advance HQ the MAILLY-MAILLET army. To Advanced sect M.V.S.	
"	" 3		To MAILLY to inspect chats to 2 Coy Div Train. To Railhead to meet 110 Remounts to	
"	" 4.		To FAMECHON to distribute remounts. M.V.S returned to FAMECHON	
"	" 5		Adv Vety Section returned to FAMECHON. To Section to make a P.M. on Horses 2682 5th Bty 4" Howitzer Brigade, put aside for 3rd Cavalry for Glanders - Enquiries of disease confirmed	
"	" 6		The completion of this last concluded investigation Reported Glanders investigation to DDVS fourth Army. Noon to-day, Division comes under Reserve Army -	
"	" 7.		Conference of Division V.O's. DDVS Reserve Army called.	
"	" 8.		Warned by DDVS - Reserve Army of attachment of VIII Corps units to this Division for administration - To MARIEUX to see Capt Cordy a/c VIII Corps. To SARTON to see Capt Thompson a/c ofs VIII Corps H.A. Group. Instructed both as to procedure	
"	" 9.		To BERTRANCOURT to see G.O.C H.A Group re mallow casting horses of 139 Battery. Dealt with Remount demand allotted surplus animals to various units - To Section FAMECHON and to 48 Divisional Train -	
"	" 10		To MUS. FAMECHON to see Mange cases. To SARTON to see V.O % H.A Group re his Mange cases - Lectured to Divisional School in afternoon.	

WAR DIARY or INTELLIGENCE SUMMARY

Army Form C. 2118.

II

Place	Date	Hour	Summary of Events and Information	Remarks and references to Appendices
HQ 46th Div.	July 11		To COIGNEUX to inspect horses of 240th Brigade. R.F.A. To Railhead to meet Remount for A.A.'s M.S.	
"	12		To FAMECHON & Sedan to see Mange Cases of 148th Inf. Brigade. To SARTON to see horses of VIIIth Corps Heavy Artillery – 25th Battery horses replete – Malcom Col. could not inspect or horses of 139th Battery.	
"	13		To SARTON to inspect horses of 139th Battery, 1st Highland, 1st Welsh, 19th, 16th and 112 Batteries Heavy Group. To THIEVRES to see horses of 1st Field Ambulance R.A.M.C. To rear Horses of 'D' Battery, 243rd Brigade – 143rd Inf. Brigade moved out.	
"	14		Conference of M.O.'s. To inspect horses of 242nd & 241st Brigades R.F.A. Wire of case of Glanders in 5th Sussex Reg't from D.D.V.S. To FAMECHON & other more of section. To SARTON to wire Town Major to wire Agate history of Glandered horse Reid belonged to him.	
"	15		Ordered to move – Made dispositions. To Army to D.D.V.S. conference.	
"	16		Enplaned my arrangements to relieving A.D.V.S. 38th Division. Marched to BOUZAINCOURT. Remt. Cavalry to locate units of Division. To WARLOY to see dent. of Green A.V.C. Ye units in this area. Section moved to FORCEVILLE.	
"	17		To SENLIS to select site for M.V.S. Lt Green case 60 horses of 5th Sussex Reg't at ALBERT. Fixed up advanced Veterinary Section at BOUZAIN COURT.	

WAR DIARY or INTELLIGENCE SUMMARY

Army Form C. 2118.

Place	Date	Hour	Summary of Events and Information	Remarks and references to Appendices
HQ Division	July 18		To Raised ACHEUX to meet 62; Remounts - To FORCEVILLE to distribute to units	
"	19		To Aboned Sebir and MVS. SENLIS. To Headquarters 145th Inf. Brigade	
"	20		To Aboned Sebir, mate Lily Sebir, and to see horse of 144th & 145th Inf. Brigades	
"	21		DDVS called. Capt Hayter ADC to X Corps H.A. G. called. To ALBERT with Lieut Grier a/v to see horse of 143rd Inf Brigade. To MVS at SENLIS. To see Cmdr of Divisional Artillery / not reached in. Saw Capt Rudd. / one a/c. obsd Lieut Grier & open his 242nd Brigade RFA yet	
"	22		detachment to duty with troops in front line. To REDOUVILLE to seek 241st Brigade now attached to 49th Division - Found Capt Nearn a.s.c. TC, brought him to HQ. and gave him charge of 143rd Inf Brigade "B" Section Doc & 2nd Field Ambulance. Found 49th Divisional Artillery into with Influenza amongst horses - Warned our CRA & took permission to move his horses to a safe spot	
"	23		Round horses of 1st 2nd & 3rd Field Companies R.E. 47th & 6th Signal Co R.E.	
"	24		145th & 145th Inf Brigades - To MVS at SENLIS. DDVS called.	
"	25		Round av horses of 240th, 242nd & 243rd Artillery Brigades. Reported bad watering arrangements to HQ.	
"	26		Round "D" Battery horses of 242nd Brigade - To Divl. Train to transport spare remounts	
"	27		Orders to move. advised O.C. Section of area to be occupied.	
"	28		Moved to DOMEUEUR by car.	

Army Form C. 2118.

WAR DIARY
or
INTELLIGENCE SUMMARY.
(Erase heading not required.)

IV

Place	Date	Hour	Summary of Events and Information	Remarks and references to Appendices
HQ Division	July 29		To BEAUVAL to see Sudan encampment & to arrow extradition of horse in case. To Rubhed VIGNACOURT to meet 107 Remounts.	
"	" 30		To ST OUEN to distribute Remounts	
"	" 31		To COULONVILLERS, MAISON ROLAND, "CRAMONT MILL to see 143rd Inf Brigade. To FRANSU, FRANQUEVILLE + HOUGENCOURT town 144th Inf Brigade	
	3 August 1916			

CBM Harris Lt. Col.
A. D. of V. S. 48th (S. M.) Division.

ADVS

Army Form C. 2118.

WAR DIARY
or
INTELLIGENCE SUMMARY.
(Erase heading not required.)

VETERINARY
48th (SM) DIVISION

Vol. 1

Place	Date	Hour	Summary of Events and Information	Remarks and references to Appendices
Headquarters Le PLOUY	Aug 1.	—	To CRAMONT and Le MÉNAGE to see 143rd Inf Brigade, more especially Brigade Machine Gun Co. lines. To ST OUEN to see 1st S.M. mobile Veterinary Schn - Lient Green are posted to DOMQUER for duty with horses in area. To Battalion Headquarters at FRANQEVILLE, LA HAYE, CRAMONT and LONGVILLERS.	
"	" 2		To LONGVILLERS to see horses of 8th Field Ambulance.	
"	" 3		To ST OUEN the a day with personnel artillery and Mobile Veterinary Schn.	
"	" 4		To DOMART to see IX Corps V.O. and Place horse IX Corps at request of A.P.M.	
"	" 5		To H.Q. & 143rd Brigade and CRAMONT area.	
"	" 6		To H.Q. & 145th Brigade. To judge at 6th Warwicks Horse Show.	
"	" 7		To R.A. units and Mobile Veterinary Schn at ST OUEN	
"	" 8		To see 6th & 7th Warwicks at MAISON ROLLAND and MESNIL-DOMQUER. Orders received for move. Lt. Green rejoins his unit 243rd Brigade R.F.A.	
Headquarters BEAUVAL	" 9		Headquarters moved to BEAUVAL. To Mobile Veterinary Schn and 48th Division from GEZAINCOURT.	
"	" 10		To Headquarters Reserve Army to see ADVS.	
"	" 11		To MARIEUX & took charger for 2nd Res. Corps. To AMPLIER and ORVILLE to see personal artillery.	
"	" 12		To MARIEUX to seek charger, but found it had gone.	
"	" 13		Headquarters moves to BOUZINCOURT. To FORCEVILLE to see Section.	

WAR DIARY or INTELLIGENCE SUMMARY

Army Form C. 2118.

Place	Date	Hour	Summary of Events and Information	Remarks and references to Appendices
Headquarters BUZINCOURT	Aug. 13		Ordered section's move to SENLIS.	
"	" 14		To SENLIS to section. To RAINCHEVAL to see B.R.V.S. Reserve Army.	
"	" 15		To see horses of 240th & 242nd Brigades R.F.A. In afternoon with A.D.V.S. to ALBERT to search for 2 horses reported abandoned by R.A.M.C. 48th Division. Discovered that the animals belonged to 3rd F.A. Water-cart.	
"	" 16		" met 85 Remounts at Railhead - to FORCEVILLE to see Remount horses of 146th Inf. Brigade with J.O.S.	
"	" 17			
"	" 18		To SENLIS to Section. Met A.D.V.S. there. To see horses of 241st Brigade R.F.A. attached to 49th W.R. Division at HEDAUVILLE - To SENLIS to Section in afternoon.	
"	" 19		To see horses of 243rd Brigade R.F.A.	
"	" 20		Quiet day - indisposed.	
"	" 21		To see horses of 144th Inf. Brigade. To SENLIS to Section.	
"	" 22		To LOUVENCOURT to see horses of 3rd Field ambulance. - To SENLIS to Section.	
"	" 23		To see mules of R.A.C., then to SENLIS to cooling pond by J.F.R. Reserve Army.	
"	" 24		To BUS with R.A.Q. m.g. 6.30 etty - To SENLIS to Section.	
"	" 25		To SENLIS to Section, to GEZAINCOURT to see Capt. Farrell A.V.C reported sick. To A.D.V.S. Reserve Army re shortage of Officers army to schemes. Put up suggestion for return of Capt. Hearn from 241st Brigade & of 49 (W.R.) Division. To see loading of Capt. Prices June horses A.V.C. at Depot of A.D.V.S. Because of possible contact with a glandered case of Canada from ROUEN Remount Depot. To see injured animals of 144th Inf. Brigade, knocked out by shell fire	

2351 Wt. W2544/1454 700,000 5/15 D. D. & L. A.D.S.S./Forms/C. 2118.

WAR DIARY
or
INTELLIGENCE SUMMARY

Army Form C. 2118.

Place	Date	Hour	Summary of Events and Information	Remarks and references to Appendices
Headquarters BOUZINCOURT	Aug. 25		Arranged to complete them to strength in horses.	
"	" 26		Round at Ja" horse ; D.D.V.S. 25th Division came & reporting me to conclude his returns of Art. Artillery of his division in my area. To Railhead to meet 49 Remounts. To FORCEVILLE to stabled to Remounts.	
"	" 27			
"	" 28		Division less Artillery moved to BERTRANCOURT, BUS, AUTHIE area.	
Headquarters BERTRANCOURT	" 29		Round round to locate units. Sent C.O. ANDERTON A.V.C. (T.C.) reported his arrival, vice Capt. Farrell A.V.C. sick. Posted him temporarily to mob. veterinary section for duty with troops in area. Ordered Cohen to move to VAUCHELLES. To BUS armd units.	
"	" 30		To PUCHEVILLERS see Section. Saw Town Major and requested him to allot a more suitable site for the unit. To see horses of 3rd Field Ambulance.	

3. Sept. 1916

C.B.M. Harris Lt. Col.
A.D. of V.S. 48th (S.M.) Division.

Army Form C. 2118.

WAR DIARY or INTELLIGENCE SUMMARY

VETERINARY
48th (S.M.) DIVISION

(Erase heading not required.)

Place	Date	Hour	Summary of Events and Information	Remarks and references to Appendices
H.Qrs 48 Division	Sep 1.	—	To see horses of 48th Divisional Tram at FORCEVILLE.	
	2		To see horses of 145th Infantry Brigade. To locate Wagon lines of 143rd Inf. Brigade.	
	3		To BOUZINCOURT to see Divisional Artillery horses. To see horses of "B" Echelon Divnl and Remounts Column at VARENNES. To Conference of A.D.V.S. Reserve Army. Strongly represented to D.D.V.S. the condition of the watering arrangements at LONG FARM, BOUZINCOURT, and asked for his action. Headquarters of Division marched to BEAUVAL.	
	4		With Camp Commandant adopting stabling for horses of Divisional Headquarters. Found all Infantry Brigades and Mobile Veterinary Section with D.A.Q.M.G. in Hospital. Arranged that he should look after horses in the BUS area when off sick list.	
	5		Round horses in BEAUVAL. Capt. G.E. Farrell A.V.C. returned to duty. To VAUCHELLES to Mobile Veterinary Section. BUS, BERTRANCOURT and FORCEVILLE. Capt. Harm A.V.C. returned to duty with 241st Brigade R.F.A. attached to 49th Division. On leaving Divisional Train.	
	6			
	7		on relief by Capt. Farrell. Office and routine. To REINCHEVAL to see D.D.V.S. Reserve Army.	
	8		Office and routine.	
	9		To VARENNES to see "B" Echelon D.A.C. and VAUCHELLES to Mobile Vety Section.	
	10		To D.D.V.S. Reserve Army, REINCHEVAL. To Railhead BELLEEGLISE to meet 72 Remounts and distributed them to Units at the station. A bad system so far as this Division is concerned and is only necessary when no responsible officer is detailed to meet Remounts.	
	12		To VAUCHELLES to see Mobile Veterinary Section	

WAR DIARY
or
INTELLIGENCE SUMMARY.
(Erase heading not required.)

Army Form C. 2118.

II

Place	Date	Hour	Summary of Events and Information	Remarks and references to Appendices
H.Q. 48th Division	Sept 13		To GEZAINCOURT to see 143rd Inf. Brigade. Schools site for Mobile Vety. Section.	
"	" 14		To VARENNES to see Capt Farrell A.V.C. Saw mules on line of march to remounts in evening.	
"	" 15		To see R.E. horses and to M.V.S. Saw horses of 145th Inf. Brigade at watering.	
"	" 16		Round horses of 145th Inf. Brigade with Brigade Transport Officer. To BOUZINCOURT and ALBERT to see Divl. Artillery units and to discuss a standard animal sent to No 7 Veterinary Hospital from D/241 Brigade R.F.A.	
"	" 17		To REINCHEVAL to No 2 DVS. Reserve Army re standard animal. Met thro D.V.S. and accompanied them to ALBERT and USNA VALLEY. To Mobile Vety. Section on return to order move to CANDAS.	
"	" 18		Mobile Veterinary Section moved to CANDAS. Division Head Quarters moved to BERNAVILLE. DDVS visited and arranged me to be ready to proceed to Meault for him during his absence sick in hospital. Round area and localised sundries. Horse accused to join Reserve Army Headquarters on 20th inst.	
"	" 19		Capts Farrell & Gaunt visited my office and their duties in present area was explained. As an V.O's bus hire air with them Artillery Brigades on the line, there is great difficulty in keeping the area covered. Left for REINCHEVAL to take over office of DDVS. Reserve Army.	
"	" 20		To Conference at "ALTOOTENCOURT". To 46th Div M.V.S. at CANDAS. To ORVILLE to see horses of 5th Corps Heavy Artillery at request of Capt Barron A.V.C. To SARTON to see Capt. Thompson A.V.C. to the Heavy Artillery horses 5th Corps & general info. prevalence of "Colic".	
H.Q. Reserve Army	" 21			

WAR DIARY or INTELLIGENCE SUMMARY

Army Form C. 2118.

III

Place	Date	Hour	Summary of Events and Information	Remarks and references to Appendices
H.Q. of Reserve Army 	Sept. 22.		To Conference at TOUTENCOURT. To see Army Commander and M.G.G.S. To ALBERT and USNA R.E. see continued water troughs at BOUZINCOURT. To see knee of D/241 Battery. 48th Divn. to BERNAVILLE and CANDAS to see 48th Division Units.	
"	Sept. 23.		To Conference at TOUTENCOURT. Instructed by M.G.C. to proceed and inspect under horse standings in area and report progress or otherwise — To V. Corps MARIEUX to obtain orders of rearrangements from C.E. To 2nd Division new standings on BOUTRE-ST LEGER road. Both poor. To A.D.V.S. 2nd Division to ask him to look into the matter. To ACHEUX and BUS to locate new standings. Called on A.D.V.S. of 18th & 39th Divisions. Put up circular memo to all A.D.V.S. to ask them to address with their suggestions in the matter of knee-standings, so as to be able to report on the subject when called upon.	
"	Sept. 24.		To Conference at TOUTENCOURT. To horse standings at BOUZINCOURT. HEDAUVILLE Road, after consulting C.E. II Corps. To AVELUY and to see knee of 5th Pontoon Park injured by shell fire. The proposed night. To CONTAY to interview "O Canadian Corps to horse standings and to see standings under construction. To BERNAVILLE & to 48th Division and CANDAS to see 48th Divn Mobile Vety. Section	
"	Sept 25		To Conference at TOUTENCOURT. Looked at the ambulance of D.V.S. orders in cleaning up & watering utensils at LONE FARM after attack of entagious disease.	
"	Sept. 26		To Conference at TOUTENCOURT. Put in report on Mules Horse Standings. To BERNAVILLE to 48th Division and CANDAS to see do Section	
"	Sept 27 Sept 28.		To Conference at TOUTENCOURT. To QUERRIEUX to see D.D.V.S. South Army. To SENLIS to see 11th Divn. M. Vety. Section and Headqs. Co. 48th Divn. Train at VARENNES.	

Army Form C. 2118.

WAR DIARY
or
INTELLIGENCE SUMMARY.
(Erase heading not required.)

Instructions regarding War Diaries and Intelligence Summaries are contained in F.S. Regs., Part II. and the Staff Manual respectively. Title pages will be prepared in manuscript.

Place	Date	Hour	Summary of Events and Information	Remarks and references to Appendices
H.Q. 48 Reserve Army	Sept 28.		To BOUZINCOURT to see C.R.A. 48th Division. To ALBERT to see V.O's 48th Divisional Artillery. To BERNAVILLE to see 48th Division and CANDAS to Mobile Veterinary Section.	
" "	Sept 29.		To Conference at TOUTENCOURT. To BERNAVILLE to 48th Division on move, via CANDAS to 48th Div. mobile Veterinary Section.	
" "	Sept 30.		To Conference at TOUTENCOURT. To MENIL to new quarters of 48th Division. Lieut W. M. John on ave reported his arrivals at 48th Divisional Headquarters for duty vice Capt Prebo Jones invalided.	

C.B.M. Mavro Lt Col
A.D.V.S. 48th Division

1. October 1916.

IV

[Stamp: A.D. of V.S. 48th (S.M.) DIVISION No. V.S. 824 Date 6/11/16]

H⁰ Qrs "Q"
48th Division

—

War Diary, Army Veterinary
Corps 48th Divn herewith
please —

CW Harris
Lt. Col.
A. D. of V. S. 48th (S. M.) Division.
6-11-16

Army Form C. 2118.

VETERINARY
48th DIVISION

Vol 19

WAR DIARY or INTELLIGENCE SUMMARY.
(Erase heading not required.)

Instructions regarding War Diaries and Intelligence Summaries are contained in F. S. Regs. Part II. and the Staff Manual respectively. Title pages will be prepared in manuscript.

Place	Date	Hour	Summary of Events and Information	Remarks and references to Appendices
H.Q.rs Reserve Army	Oct. 1	—	To Conference at Army "Q" office. To H.Q. 48th Division for Office and to pick up newly joined officer Lieut Wm Jackson AVC, to take him to 240th Brigade R.F.A. ALBERT to which he is attached vice Capt Pude Jones AVC sick and invalided to Base.	
"	Oct. 2		To Conference at Army "Q" office. To 2nd Canadian Mobile Vety Section with DDR Reserve Army and Head Quarters Heavy Group R.G.A. ALBERT. To 48th Division for office work.	
"	Oct. 3.		Handed over to D.D.V.S. Reserve Army on his return from sick leave, and round Headquarters 48th Division. — Round H.Q. 2nd and Divisional Signal Co. horses.	
"	Oct. 4		Sent in Glanders Report to A.D.V.S. Third Army, a brief resumé, to acquaint him with facts connected with the outbreak, when the Division was under Reserve Army. To Mobile Vety section and round the horses — Capt Green AVC reported that 8	
"	Oct. 5.		cases of Contagious Influenza had been left in stables occupied by a unit of 46th Divisional Artillery, and the Sergt. AVC in charge reported that 40 cases had occurred in those stables. To WARLINCOURT to locate Divisional Artillery horses.	
"	Oct. 6.		Conference of Divisional V.O's. All present. To meet 83 Remounts for Division at railhead, SAULTY-LARBRET. Train due 13 hours late, so I detailed Capt. Gaunt AVC to meet Remounts —	
"	Oct. 7.		To WARLINCOURT to distribute 84 Remounts to Section units. To Mobile Vety Section at WARLINCOURT.	
"	Oct. 8.		To Divisional Amm." Column re disinfection of stabling. Put up letter to "Q" asking that disinfection of stabling be carried out.	

WAR DIARY or INTELLIGENCE SUMMARY

Army Form C. 2118.

Place	Date	Hour	Summary of Events and Information	Remarks and references to Appendices
ADS 48th Div	Oct. 9		To see horses of 143rd Infantry Brigade. 8 cases of Contagious Influenza reported by Capt Darling a/c in 3rd Pontoon Park R.E. Reported to D.D.V.S. 3rd Army.	
"	Oct. 10		With San. tanks to select photo site of Mobile Vety Section. 17th Division having moved out present one. Rode to GAUDIEMPRE. Saw A.D.V.S. 17th Divn and arranged sites for Advanced Collecting Posts in the event of fighting.	
"	Oct. 11		To Mob Section and both Capt Gaunt sure to new sites for M.V.S. in GAUDIEMPRE. Captain Darling & Lieut. Jackson called.	
"	Oct. 12		To SOUASTRE to reconnoitre sites for Advanced Collecting Post. To GAUDIEMPRE to Section. Took Capt Gaunt to see No 3rd Cos. 48th Divisional Train and saw horses of Nos 3rd Cos. 48th Divisional Train.	
"	Oct. 13		To Railhead SAULTY-LARBRET to meet 62 Remounts for the Division.	
"	Oct. 14		To WARLINCOURT to see hibried Remounts to Units of the Division. To inspect horses of No 2 Co. Divisional Train with O.C. Train. To H.Q. 7. Corps. D.A.S.	
"	Oct. 15		Round Headquarters horses.	
"	Oct. 16		To 7th Worcesters HUMBERCOURT to see horses and inspect strength of horses. Ho unit having collected some surplus. Appln for 10 days leave. Granted from 17" inst to 26" inst. Handed over office to Capt Farrell A.V.C.	
"	Oct. 17		Correspondence. Left for BOULOGNE - Capt. Gaunt called.	
"	Oct. 18		Correspondence. F Remounts arrived at WARLINCOURT to police patrol	

WAR DIARY or INTELLIGENCE SUMMARY

Army Form C. 2118.

Place	Date	Hour	Summary of Events and Information	Remarks and references to Appendices
HQ 48th Divn.	Oct 19		Correspondence. Lieut. Jackson A.V.C. called.	
"	20		Correspondence. Conference. Capt Gould absent on duty	
"	21		Headquarters Division moved to DOULLENS	
"	22		Correspondence	
"	23		Headquarters Division moved to BAIZIEUX. Mobile Veterinary Section about to move to TALMAS	
"	24		Rejoined Division on recall from leave.	
"	25		Round HQ 143 Bde. To HQ 6th Fourth Army to see A.D.V.S.	
"	26		Divisional units on move. Recalled Capt. Darling to duty with Infantry & R.E. units in forward area. Sand	
"	27		Put up new A O/c units reporting to this office. Particulars of horses left with civilians - Sand a/c Mg. re clipping. Capt Farrell called. Saw Capt Gould and Mobile Veterinary Section. Round horses of Divisional Signal Co. To Mobile Veterinary Section - Capts. Farrell, Gould called.	
"	28		Round HQ 6ro horses. To ALBERT and our next camp forward at MILLENCOURT.	
"	29		To BECOURT to inspect site of 15th Division Mobile Vety Section and visited O.C. 48th Division Section & proceed to inspect it as to its suitability, so to me, as it is a summer site only & not suitable for winter.	
"	30		To ADVS 49th Division. To MILLENCOURT Camp. Capt. Darling reports his recall.	
"	31		Ht. Q. moved to MILLENCOURT Camp. Capt. Darling reports his arrival.	

1/Nov./1916

C.B.M. Harris
Lt Col.
ADVS 48th Division

WAR DIARY or INTELLIGENCE SUMMARY

Army Form C. 2118.

ADVS VETERINARY 48th (S.M.) DIVISION

Vol 20

Place	Date	Hour	Summary of Events and Information	Remarks and references to Appendices
48th Division	Nov 1916		Mobile Veterinary section moved to ALBERT (E4d.1.8). Capt Darling noted and the work required in the area was explained to him.	
	" 2.		Divisional HQ under orders to move. Sent on office to LOZENGE WOOD.	
	" 3.		Divisional HQ moved to LOZENGE WOOD Camp. To see ADVS 50th Division as to care of neighbouring units.	
	" 4.		Walked round camps.	
	" 5.		No office arrangements having been made for me, consulted AA & QMG who kindly allowed me a corner in the 'Q' office.	
	" 6.		To locate CHAPES SPUR Camp where infantry transport horses of the Division are encamped. Located wagon lines of 102nd & 103rd Bdes. R.F.A. (23rd Division). Lieut Carroll AVC of 10 B. Brigade R.F.A. called. The 23rd Divisional Artillery is under the administration of 48th Division. 1 Troop. Duke of Lancasters Own Yeomanry arrived on staff for draft duties.	
	" 7.		Saw the following horses from 4 Cavalry Brigade - 13 to 143 Brigade, 15 to 144 Inf Bde. and 13 to 145 Inf Bde.	
	" 8.		To see DDVS Fourth Army. 2 men of 1/1 S.M. Mobile Vety Section reported sick with "German measles" and sent placed in quarantine. Wrote asking ADVS 1st Division if he would allow the MVS to carry on. Wired that information to DDVS Fourth Army.	

WAR DIARY or INTELLIGENCE SUMMARY

Army Form C. 2118.

Place	Date	Hour	Summary of Events and Information	Remarks and references to Appendices
H.Q.'d'S 46th Div.	Nov 9.		To see horses of 1st & 2nd Cos R.E. – 9th (Pioneer) Battn Gordon Highlanders. 74th & 2nd Co R.E. all in very good condition. Two mules Capt Darling to take charge of and later into. To CHAPES SPUR to see draught Transport horses of 6th Lancasters with 9/o Battalion.	
"	Nov 10.		To meet 76 Remounts at Railhead at EDGEHILL. To ALBERT to discuss the Remounts to units. To see O/C 1st Divisional Train re loss of 2 mules from the Remount lines. To inspect horses of 4th Cavalry Brigade. Orders for fresh purchases to 1st Field Ambulance at LOZENGE WOOD CAMP. Named Capt. Darling to be ready to take up his quarters at CHAPES SPUR. Capt Baumet arr. c/o 1st S.M. M.V.S. called.	
"	Nov 11.		Inspected an intending Bicycle & Machine Gun Co's horses at CHAPES SPUR. Inspected an intending Bicycle detachment and referred on them to "c" for information of horses of Cavalry detachment and referred on them to "c" for information of Corps. Arranged that Capt. Darling are elsewhere with B.To. 143rd Inf. Bde.	
"	Nov 12.		Capt Darling are moved to CHAPES SPUR. To CONTALMAISON to see 1st Field Ambulance – Particulars showing scheme for "picked up Posts" sent out to 1/O 143rd Inf. Brigade.	
"	Nov 13.		To V.63 for return. To CHAPES SPUR to see B.TO 146th Inf. Brigade.	

WAR DIARY or INTELLIGENCE SUMMARY.

Army Form C. 2118.

Place	Date	Hour	Summary of Events and Information	Remarks and references to Appendices
H.Q.D 46 Division	Nov.14		To ALBERT to see O/C M.V.S. and A.D.V.S. 1st Division. Suspected knees of 162nd Brigade R.F.A. of 23rd Division at LOZENGE WOOD.	
"	" 15		J. Conference at A.D.V.S. Fourth Army.	
"	" 16		Forward depôt & sergeants arrive.	
"	" 17		Suspected knees of 104 Brigade R.F.A (23rd Division). To CHAPE'S SPUR to see Infantry transport horses.	
"	" 18		Capt. Straley 21st Lancers attached to this office for one day. Probable him on Veterinary as an N.C. station of. To see standings of 23rd Divisional Ammunition Column & horse lines of 74 C.R.E. and 1st 2nd C.R.E (46th Div) and 9th	
"	" 19		(Rover) Battalion Gordon Highlanders at FRICOURT FARM, Capt. Grant and darling cattle. Capt. Starkey R.A.V.C. 9th 23rd Division Amm & Column cared. Explained him A.D.V.S. memo re Pastilline showing for "picked up nails". To CONTAL MAISON to see standings for horse of 1st Field Ambulance.	
"	" 20		To CHAPE'S SPUR to see the V.O.4/c who showed me his shoeing for "picked up nails". Orders received to move 1st S.M. M.V.S. As E5c central.	
"	" 21			

WAR DIARY
INTELLIGENCE SUMMARY

Army Form C. 2118.

IV

Place	Date	Hour	Summary of Events and Information	Remarks and references to Appendices
H.Q.V. 46th Division	Nov. 22	—	To CHIPPES SPUR to inspect Brigade Transport horses attached to 74th F.Co. R.E. Inspected horses shod for prevention of "picks up nails". Capt. Starkey R.A.V.C. called.	
"	" 23	—	To see A.D.V.S. 1st Division.	
"	" 24	—	To QUERRIEU & to see A.D.V.S. Fourth army. — To St GRATIEN to see O/c Divisional School, and O/c Horses Veterinary Section. 23rd Division — To 19 S.M. mvd at HEBERT. Buildings not finished and no roofing yet supplied for stables.	
"	" 25	—	Orderly of Augeren "referred amongst horses of 104th Brigade R.F.A. at ST. GRATIEN. — Warned A.D.V.S. this information.	
"	" 26	—	To ST GRATIEN to inspect horses reported affected with Augeren. Found Brigade had moved to BASIEUX. Drove there and inspected all horses of Brigade. To DRIVE to arrange a supply of lime to making Col. Biedulph. O/c for throwing. To see G.O.C. 23rd D.n. & anything to report escort & my inspection. To St GRATIEN to arrange about making of Column Sulph. Solution for dressing Augeren Cases. — To see A.D.V.S. Fourth army & suggest that A.D.V.S.	
"	" 27	—	15th Division mvd at BASIEUX should supervise the dressing of the horses in 102nd Brigade R.F.A. He agreed. — Visited 12 S.M. mvd at E.S.C. Andre.	

WAR DIARY or INTELLIGENCE SUMMARY.

Army Form C. 2118.

V

Place	Date	Hour	Summary of Events and Information	Remarks and references to Appendices
HQ 46 Division	Nov. 28		Letter received from ADVS. 15th Division, agreeing to superintend dressing of horses of 162nd Brigade R.F.A. on no further from DDVS Fourth Army.	
"	29		To Cohnie on "Horse mastership & stable management" at Divisional School. ST. GRATIEN. To MVS of ESc Central. Capt.& Pride Jones arrived at —	
"	30		ALBERT on return from sick leave — Saw 75 Tarpaulins safely deposited at more to the purposes of 305 F.A.Brig. — To CHAPPES SPAD in afternoon.	
	1-12-16.			

C. M. W. Kennes
Lt. Col. ADVS.
46th Division

Army Form C. 2118.

WAR DIARY
or
INTELLIGENCE SUMMARY.
(Erase heading not required.)

VETERINARY
48th (S.M.) Division

Place	Date	Hour	Summary of Events and Information	Remarks and references to Appendices
Hd Qrs 48th Division	1916 Sept 2		Correspondence. To see watering arrangements of 23rd Divisional Artillery. To ALBERT to see O.C. 48th Divl. Train.	
"	" 3		To meet 66 Remounts at Railhead (EDGEHILL). Very bad show, owing to unwells having 6 delirium and take over their horses at the Station	
"	" 4		To CHIMPES SPUR to inspect all details by Brigade Transport horses. To see horses of 2nd/1st 3rd Field Companies R.E. at CHIMPES SPUR. To see Divl. Signal Co. horses at LOZENGE WOOD. Correspondence. G.O.C. Division noted "C" Office and expressed his anger at seeing some horses of 143rd Inf. Brigade clipped. Saw 48th Divl. Artillery march in. Horses had marched 20 miles, and on the whole looked well.	
"	" 5			
"	" 6		23rd Divl Artillery left. Sent orders to Capt Jackson AVC from A.D.V.S. Fourth Army to report himself to ADVS. 50th Division for duty, in relief by Capt Prade-Jones, returning from sick leave. To Coal Wagon horses of 48th Divl. Artillery. Capt Prade-Jones reported his return & took over 240th Brigade R.F.A. from Lieut. Jackson, AVC. Lieut W.M. Jackson AVC left Division	
"	" 7		To Divl. Mobile Rly. Section. To HdQrs 48th Divl. Train. B.T.O. RVC let Base notes re mange in two of the horses	
"	" 8		Capt Prade-Jones and Darling called. Explained to former the Premature showing Scheme for Picked up mules. To CONTALMAISON to see watering of 240 Brigade R.F.A. horses.	
"	" 9			

WAR DIARY or INTELLIGENCE SUMMARY

Place	Date	Hour	Summary of Events and Information	Remarks and references to Appendices
HQ 48th Division	Dec 9		Put up cases to ODVS Fourth Army, re outbreak of contagious disease in forward area and starting twenty watering arrangements in forward area. Asked him to do so to inspect with me.	
"	" 10		To FRICOURT FARM. To see 1st Field Co. R.E. horses. To BAZIEUX to see "A" Camp prepared for 48th Div. Artillery horses. To FREUTENCOURT to see 48th D.A.C. To BETHENCOURT to see Town Major re billetting of 242nd Brigade horses.	
"	" 11		To Meric Vely Section to arrange about billetting HQ's Brigade horses, on move of the Division. White ADVS 15th Division to see me, re veterinary arrangements for Division in the line. The 15th Division relieves us.	
"	" 12		To FRICOURT FARM to see ADVS 17th Division, and wrote over my arrangements at the FARM.	
"	" 13		To MAMETZ WOOD. Saw V.O. 7c 240th Brigade. ADVS 15th Division no less to be arranged move of leopard made rely section.	
"	" 14		Ordered Capt Durling a/c to move with B.T.D. 143rd Inf Brigade. Advised Capt Farrar that the care of at units would cease on our relief by 16th Division.	
"	" 14		On 16th instant. Round horses of Div Signal Co. R.E.	
"	" 15		To Lecture on "Horse mastership & Stable management" at Divisional School, SGRATEN.	

WAR DIARY or INTELLIGENCE SUMMARY

Army Form C. 2118.

Place	Date	Hour	Summary of Events and Information	Remarks and references to Appendices
HQn 48th Division	Dec. 16.		Division Headqrs. moved to ALBERT. M.V.S. moved to BAZIEUX.	
	" 17.		Capt. Darling & Green called. To inspect horses of 48th Divl. Train. All in very good condition and showing the weather conditions well.	
	" 18.		To Railhead (EDGEHILL) to meet 96 Remounts, all for artillery. To inspect horses of A/240 Bde. R.F.A. at Dell's Farm.	
	" 19.		Arrange veterinary supervision with Capt. Farrell, R.A.V.C. of and Green. Inspected transport horses of 144th Inf. Bde. with of Brigadier Colonel Harman &c. Capt. Darling left on leave. To Wagon lines of 143rd Inf. Brigade.	
	" 20.		To lines of C/240. Brigade with V.O.'s.	
	" 21.		To BAZIEUX to see Sebin. To Hd. lines.	
	" 22.		To 15th D.A. meat Rly. Sidim to see our Hd Hd horses which are stabled there. Arranged to move them.	
	" 23.		To DD VS' Conference at HQ. Fourth Army.	
	" 24.		To BAZIEUX to see Sebin.	
	" 25.		To inspect Transport lines of 143rd Inf. Bde. Reported C.H.R. Brigade. Also unsatisfactory condition of horses of 5th R. Warwick Regiment.	

WAR DIARY

Army Form C. 2118.

IV

Place	Date	Hour	Summary of Events and Information	Remarks and references to Appendices
H.Q. 48 Division	Mar. 26		BECOURT. To inspect horses of 143rd Inf Bde at REVIGNY	
"	" 27		To BAZIEUX to obtain several ambulance horses of S.S. LETACH & Mrs. to proceed on chief no long. Instructor to School of Farriery ABBEVILLE. To BAMENCOURT to see 48th D.A.C.	
"	" 28		To BAMENCOURT to see 2/1 Bde R.F.A. To FRETIENCOURT to see 48th D.A.C. To BAZIEUX to Section and to see Town Major, with a view to preventing occupation of Section Stablings by horses of 48 Divisional Train.	
"	" 29		To BAZIEUX to Section. To see HR horses and 48th Divl Signal Co horses.	
"	" 30		To H.Q. horses. To see horses of 3rd Field Ambulance. Rams & horses not but very badly accommodated. To recommend relation cordwin & organise a move to a better spot. To see Artillery horses at DOLL'S FARM. Capt. Col. Roberts 48 DAC. Capt Farrah are called.	
"	" 31		To see 2/1/18 Fourth Army. Spoke to D.V.S. on telephone re a relief to Capt Farrell.	

C. Bru Harris M/C
A.D.V.S. 48th Division
3/4/17.

WAR DIARY
or
INTELLIGENCE SUMMARY.

(Erase heading not required.)

Army Form C. 2118.

ADVeterinary
48th DIVISION

Instructions regarding War Diaries and Intelligence Summaries are contained in F. S. Regs., Part II. and the Staff Manual respectively. Title pages will be prepared in manuscript.

A.D. of V.S.
No. V.S. 915
Date 15/2/17
48th (S.M.) DIVISION

Place	Date	Hour	Summary of Events and Information	Remarks and references to Appendices
Headquarters 48th Division	Jany 1st		Division Headquarters moved to BAIZIEUX. To WARLOY to see horses of 2nd Field Ambulance R.A.M.C.	
"	2nd		To BEHENCOURT to see horses of 290th Brigade R.F.A. with Y/CRA and VO/c Capt Rice Jones. "B" Battery horses in a bad state.	
"	3rd		To M.V.S. to see Sergt Lucas (1st S.M. Mt.B) with reference to his application for a commission. Capt Hearn are reported his return from leave. Capt Darling asse returned from leave. To BRESLE to see H.Q & 145th Infantry Brigade	
"	4th		Took over command of Section vice Capt Gaunt are proceeding on leave from 6th to 16th instant	
"	5th		To Lechon and round H.Q horses. Sergt Lucas (1st S.M. Mt.B) come with me to interview A.A. re. reply to his application for a commission. Attended BOO's Conference	
"	6th		To DDVS' Conference at A.H.Q. Wrote C.R.A. re exchange of mts between Capts Hearn & Green.	
"	7th		To FRECHENCOURT to endeavour to arrange transfers for m/Lieuts (?). Saw V/oc 48th D.A.C. Wrote Col Browne % 48th D.A.C. on leave on the question	

WAR DIARY or INTELLIGENCE SUMMARY

Army Form C. 2118.

Place	Date	Hour	Summary of Events and Information	Remarks and references to Appendices
Headquarters 48th Division	Jany 8		Headquarters moved to HALLENCOURT	
"	9		Reported move by wire to 31 S. Jn & Army. Rode out to village looking for 6 horses – Saw Capt Darling and desired him not to disturb. Wired Capt Fowell who had taken over command of Sedan that as soon as the horses cured and to be found at FRECHEN COURT, the unit should remain at BAIZIEUX and he was to visit every day. Capt Darling advised mange amongst horses of H.Q. 145th Infy. Brigade	
"	10		Round H.Q. horses. To MONET to locate 5th R Warwickshire Regt. Saw Brigade Transport Officer – applied for 10 days leave	
"	11		Round H.Q. horses. To CITERNE to see horses of 4th R Berks Regt	
"	12		With Capt Darling to AIRAINES and ALLERY. Found in former a Depôt for French sick horses – Interviewed Commandant and Officier Veterinaire in charge. The latter appeared from the volunteer state of affairs with which he was dealing and I decided that all horses of this Division should be moved out. Issued necessary instructions	

Place	Date	Hour	Summary of Events and Information	Remarks and references to Appendices
Headquarters 48th Division	July	12th	To ALLERY. Found horses infested with mange and knew of the 33rd Division, collected suffering from the same complaint. Endeavoured to arrange to have horses removed at.	
"	"	13th	Capt Hearn arrived 24/1st Brigade R.F.A. reported by Adj, a Veterinary case of glanders in a mule at CONTAY MAISON - Wondering to give no doubt of his test. Army team received sanction & asked 33rd South Army to arrange supervision of "B" Battery & glanders was found & one to	
"	"	14th	Round the horses - No line from Capt Hearn.	
"	"	15th	To meet D.D.V.S. Fourth Army at AIROINES - With him to ABBEVILLE Via D.I.S. BEF	
"	"	16th	Left on 10 days leave. Capt Farrell arrived to take over office	
"	"	17th	Routine - Sewardanly & S.S.O. on his inspection & stabling & water	
"	"	18th	Frigate on the new area - Capt Darling called Routine	
"	"	19th	To PONT REMY to see 1st Field Co R.E. - to HUCHENVILLE to see horses of H.B. Gloster Regt at to report of OC this had	

WAR DIARY
or
INTELLIGENCE SUMMARY.
(Erase heading not required.)

Army Form C. 2118.

Place	Date	Hour	Summary of Events and Information	Remarks and references to Appendices
Headquarters 48th Division	Jany 19		reported back in am. I could find but little wrong 6 a [?] could'nt only. To BALLEUL to see 5th Royal Sussex Horses.	
"	"	20.	To D.D.V.S'. Conference at ALBERT and from there on reconnaissance in new area.	
"	"	21.	Routine. Wired Capt Gaunt to send Sergt Lucas and 4 men with the 2 wheeled float to FONTAINE to report to O/c 2nd Co 48th Div^{nal} Train, for orders - this detachment is to deal with the evacuation of sick animals of the Division in the area	
"	"	22.	Routine. Submitted report on my inspection of stabling and watering arrangements in the new area. To D.D.V.S. and H.Q. Division. Capt Darling called	
"	"	23	Routine. Sergt Lucas called to report his arrival at FONTAINE the previous evening.	
"	"	24th	To meet 99 Remounts at HANGEST. Capt Darling met the train but had only detrained a few animals, so units failed to send cavalry halters & chains	

A 5834 Wt. W4973/1687 750,000 8/16 D. D. & L. Ltd. Forms/C.2118/13.

Army Form C. 2118.

WAR DIARY
or
INTELLIGENCE SUMMARY.
(Erase heading not required.)

Place	Date	Hour	Summary of Events and Information	Remarks and references to Appendices
Headquarters 48th Division	Jany 25		To FONTAINE to distribute 16 Rulers & 13 miles not extended yesterday to the horses of 1st Fresh Coy R.E. at PONT REMY - Wired Section to move to CERISY with R.Q.	
"	26		To 144th Infantry Brigade. Sergt Sweno called. Arranged with him to conduct 7 sick horses to CERISY.	
"	27		ABBEVILLE by road - Section moved to CERISY.	
"	28		Division HQ moved to MERICOURT	
"	29		Routine. Capt Darling called	
"	30		Routine	
"	31		10½ & 240 Brigade R.F.A. reported by wire that a case of STOMATITIS CONTAGIOSA had been found in their "C" Battery and that disinfection and all precautionary measures had been carried out. Reported same to ADVS Fourth Army. Cap. Green called.	

10/2/17

C.B. Matthews MRC
ADVS 48th D.S.

WAR DIARY / INTELLIGENCE SUMMARY

ADVS 48 / VETERINARY I / 48 (SM) DIVISION
Vol 77

Place: H.Q. A.D.V.S. 48th Division

Date	Hour	Summary of Events and Information	Remarks
February 1917 1		Decided that 2nd Brigade R.F.A. horses should not water at the general watering troughs owing to their case of CONTAGIOUS STOMATITIS.	2, 3
" 2		Routine – Capt. Green called. M.V.S moved to CAPPY.	
" 3		Div. H.Q. moved to CAPPY.	
" 4		To inspect 240th Brigade R.F.A Waggon lines – To 1st Field Ambulance R.A.M.C. Capt Hearn ave. Called. Mange reported in 3rd Field Ambulance R.A.M.C. Directed Capt Darling ave to investigate and report.	
" 5		Routine. Capt Pride Jones ave. called.	
" 6		Routine. Capt Darling & Green called.	
" 7		To 'B' Echelon D.A.C. A.D.V.S. returned to duty.	
" 8		To M.O. to report return and round H.Q. horses – To 'A' Echelon D.A.C. To 145th 3rd Brigade. Capt Darling ave. called.	
" 9		Capt. Pride Jones, Gaunt & Darling ave called.	
" 10		Compiled and despatched War Diary. To M.O. Capt Gaunt, Pride Jones & Farrell ave. called. – To inspect Sedm. Not satisfied with Sun section Capt Gaunt up re: outbreak of mange in 474 F.Co. R.E. Capt. Farrell reported a case of STOMATITIS in 4th /B" Yorks Reg. Reported both facts by wire to A.D.V.S Fourth Army –

A.D. of V.S. No. VS.939 53/1
(M) DIVISION

Army Form C. 2118.

WAR DIARY
or
INTELLIGENCE SUMMARY.
(Erase heading not required.)

II

Instructions regarding War Diaries and Intelligence Summaries are contained in F.S. Regs., Part II. and the Staff Manual respectively. Title pages will be prepared in manuscript.

Place	Date	Hour	Summary of Events and Information	Remarks and references to Appendices
HQ 48th Division	February 11		With Serj. Bailey R.V.C. to see cases of STOMATITIS. DDVS Fourth Army called. Took him to see STOMATITIS and MANGE cases at FROISSY.	
"	"	12	To 46 D.A.C. With Lt Bonnett Officer Interpreter to see some virulent cases of Mange amongst French horses. Asked O.C. Service Ruthier Armee Francaise to take care to keep animals separate and to water them from tins. To HQ horses.	
"	"	13	To M.V.S. — To see horses of 248th Brigade R.F.A. with Capt Pike Jones VO 1/c. — Reported to CRA the very poor condition of the horses of "D"/240 and put up suggestions with a view to improvement. Capt Farrell called and inspected 3 mange cases of STOMATITIS. Reported same by letter to DDVS Fourth Army — Looked horses of 241 Bde. R.F.A. & Backs B.F. 145 Inf. Bde. To ordering horse glasses of 240 & 241 Brigades R.F.A.	
"	"	14	To DDVS Conference HQ Fourth Army.	
"	"	15	To see horses of 241st Brigade R.F.A. Visit Capt Green VO 1/c. To FROISSY with OC MVS (Capt Grant) to see horse isol. for his selection — Wrote Rev RAMC a nice suitable office near than at present. No satisfactory results — Capt Farrell reported 3 more cases of STOMATITIS in 4th Bn. Glo'ster Regt., making 7 in all to date. Reported this by wire to DDVS Fourth Army. To District MO Gt. Gorgian Saiollon for mouth & nostril swabs of reuniter —

WAR DIARY
or
INTELLIGENCE SUMMARY.
(Erase heading not required.)

Army Form C. 2118.

Place	Date	Hour	Summary of Events and Information	Remarks and references to Appendices
HQ'rs 48th Division	February 15		To see CRA re faults in stable management in A/241 Brigade.	
"	16		Conference of VO's. Two STOMATITIS cases with 2nd VO's.	
"	17		Confined to room - Bad cold	
"	18		To H.Q. horses and 2nd Bn Headquarters - Cap' Darling new C.O. charge of 180th Tunnelling Co R.E.	
"	19		Round horses of 145th Inf Brigade. Saw Capt Farrell regarding 2nd Co horse of 3rd Field Ambulance at ECLUSIER. Section moved to FROISSY. Inspected at horses of M.M.P.	
"	20		To see horses of 2nd Field Ambulance. To HQ 48th Divl Train to advise on the infection of lating. To Rachdahl CHUIGNES with O.C. Train - Section evacuated horses to day from LE PLATEAU	
"	21		To CHATEAU Cord horses of Div H.Q. - Proposed lines for squad Co of impartial went to O.C.	
"	22		To H.Q. - D.D.R. Fourth army invited and sent 7 horses of Train, 4 mules of D.A.C. and 1 H.D. of 5th Glosters are for view - to FROISSY to see M.V.P.	
"	23		To HQ. to ECLUSIER to see horses of 43rd Inf. Brigade. Conference of VO's.	
"	24		To see horses of M.M.P. Reported 2 more cases of STOMATITIS in 4 B. Glosters Regt.	

WAR DIARY or INTELLIGENCE SUMMARY

Army Form C. 2118.

Place	Date	Hour	Summary of Events and Information	Remarks and references to Appendices
H.Q. 48th Division	February 25	10 A.M.	To FROISSY to see horses of M.V.S. and manage cases in 474th Field Co. R.E. Capt. Price Jones on leave.	
"	26		To ECLUSIER to see horses of A.A.C. 144" Inf. Brigade and horses of 8th B.R. Warwick Regt.	
"	27		To FRISE to see horses of 5th B. R. Warwick Regt. To CHIPILLY to see Brig. Ato horses. To H.Q. Division to arrange for Capt. of telegram to convalescents to work in MDS for a few days. To ECLUSIER to see STOMATITIS cases with Capt. Ferrell — Saw 2nd Field Ambulance watering parade — very faulty and spoke to OC.	
"	28		To D.D.V.S. Conference H.Q. Fourth Army	

5/3/17.

John Harris Lt Col
ADVS 48th Division

WAR DIARY or INTELLIGENCE SUMMARY

Army Form C. 2118.

ADVS No 1 VETERINARY 48th (S.M.) Division Vol 1

Place	Date	Hour	Summary of Events and Information	Remarks and references to Appendices
H.Q.'rs 48th Division	1917 March 1		To H.Q. Division at OLYMPE, re distribution of surplus horses of Division. To H.Q. horses in evening. To H.Q. 144th Inf. Brigade, and to see horses of 145th Inf. Brigade. St Q.S.	
"	" 2		To H.Q. OLYMPE - Conference of V.O's. - D.D.V.R. Fourth Army called - To M.V.S. at FROISSY. To cast various mules of 242nd Brigade. R.F.A.	
"	" 3		To see horses of the Oxfords and 4th Royal Berks Transport. To H.Q. at OLYMPE re strength return of horses - Capt. Green returned from leave.	
"	" 4		Round all units of Infantry Brigades with D.A.D.V.S. adjusting matter of surplus H.Q. horses - Round Brig. H.Q. horses at CHALAIS CAPPY. Case of STOMATITIS contagiosa reported in M.T.S. transferred from 144 M.S.C.o. Reported by wire to D.D.V.S. Fourth Army.	
"	" 5		Parade of all surplus horses of Division as arranged. D.D.V.R. Fourth Army for instructions. Took Serg! Lucas (1st S.M.M.V.S.) to O/c 4/5 Royal Berks for attachment to Battalion for 10 days with a view to his obtaining a Commission	
"	" 6		Capt! Gaunt, Pride Jones and Green called - Further case of STOMATITIS reported in 7th Worcesters. Admit D.D.V.S.	
"	" 7		To ECLUSIER with V.O. of 144th Inf. Brigade, to see 7th Worcester horse. Standings - Inspected water trough and upheld its filthy condition to a.a. reg.	

WAR DIARY
or
INTELLIGENCE SUMMARY.
(Erase heading not required.)

Army Form C. 2118.

Place	Date	Hour	Summary of Events and Information	Remarks and references to Appendices
HQ.P 48th Div.an.	March 7.		who directed me to write my own orders - Write accordingly to HQ. 144th Inf. Brigade.	
	8.		To HQ OLYMPE and to see HQ horses at Chateau CAPPY. Shaw sick and heads handed at 3 p.m., and BSR. Fort Army inspected and evacuated all to not to L.O.C. 10 Riders and 9 Pack horses sent to M.V.S. for evacuation.	
	9.		Conference NCO's. Rebuked Capt. Farrell o/charge of 144th Inf. Brigade by Cpl. Green, with a view to more efficient handling for suppression of contagious diseases in 144th Inf. Brigade.	
	10.		To HQ's at OLYMPE. Capt. Green called.	
	11.		To Transport Lines of 144th Inf. Brigade with D.A.A. and Q. and shew him about 1 regined in the matter of disinfection of their infected lines. (STOMATITIS CONTAG.IOSA) Round horses of 48th D.A.C. with O/C - Found sick lines much Sergt Robert are. and Sergt Dryburgh are unsatisfactory, and write complaint to VOY (Capt. Farrell)	
	12		To FROISSY to see horses of M.V.S. To see Mange cases of 474 Co.R.E. Round A, B, & C Batteries 240 Brigade R.F.a. with C.R.A.	
	13.		To FROISSY to see horses of 474. Co.R.E. and to FRISE to see horses of 476. Co.R.E. To Chabai CAPPY to see C.R.E. & O.C. 474 Field Co. R.E. To H.Q. OLYMPE to report on airplane HQ horses of Division.	

WAR DIARY or INTELLIGENCE SUMMARY

Army Form C. 2118.

III

Place	Date	Hour	Summary of Events and Information	Remarks and references to Appendices
H.Q.R. 48th Division	March 14.		To H.Q. OLYMPE to report failure to put out of bounds the watering trough of 144" Inf. Brigade. Capt. Farrell left on leave. 15th to 25th inst. Capt. Darling instructed to act for him. Lt. Gossett attached Staff, came to me for instruction in veterinary administration.	
"	15		To H.Q. OLYMPE. To ECLUSIER. To see Sergt. Lucas who is sick in hospital. Round horses of 3rd Field Ambulance, and H.Q. 145th Inf. Brigade. Round horses of 1st Field Ambulance. Round H.Q. horses at Chateau CAPPY. To see C.R.E. accompanying him & now his H.Q. horses to Chateau for better supervision. Capt. Darling also drew his attention to what I considered to be faulty handling of mange outbreak in 3rd Field Ambulance. Capt. Green called re STOMATITIS cases. Rec'd 6 Feed Cashier Recs 16. 75. ('14.) representing cost of instruments demanded on repayment by O.C. M.V.S. Round H.Q. 12.S. horses.	
"	16		To H.Q. OLYMPE. Conference of V.O's. Capt. Hearn was not present, away to his Brigade preparing for a move.	
"	17		To Chateau CAPPY to see M.O. horse. Then to HERBECOURT to see horse of 5th Sussex - transferred 5 LDS and 2 mules surplus of St. Lucers to 143rd Inf. Brigade.	

WAR DIARY
or
INTELLIGENCE SUMMARY.
(Erase heading not required.)

Army Form C. 2118.

Place	Date	Hour	Summary of Events and Information	Remarks and references to Appendices
H.Q.ts 48th Div.	March 17		To OZEMPE H.Q.R. to call up O.D.R. Fourth Army. He reported shortness of horses in the Division. Took papers in charge of drunkenness against Corporal Taylor 1st S.M. M.P.8 and applied for a cmt. martial.	
"	18		To H.Q. to submit application for special leave for Private Lamb 1st S.M. M.P.8 on account of the death of his aged mother - O.D.R. Fourth Army informed that no remounts were available.	
"	19		To DDVS Conference H.Q. Fourth Army - To see O/C 242" Bde R.F.A. re-mounting the Division next morning.	
"	20		To H.Q. OZEMPE for orders. To see B.T.O. 144" Inf. Brigade re surplus horses. To see horses of Service Rentier, L'armée Francaise, and report their condition to O/C Service Rentier, VILLARS BRETONNEUX. To Château CAPPY to see H.Q. horses.	
"	21		To enable me to see conditions of Division horses, ambulance traffic on day on SOMME Pontoon Bridge.	
"	22		Capt. Green Arv. over to forward area. Capt. Pride-Jones Darling called. Put ladder in charge of 144" Inf. Brigade.	

WAR DIARY
or
INTELLIGENCE SUMMARY.
(Erase heading not required.)

Army Form C. 2118.

Place	Date	Hour	Summary of Events and Information	Remarks and references to Appendices
H.Q. 48" Division	March 23		Conference of M.O.'s. To BIACHES, HALLE, and PERONNE on reconnaissance for site of M.V.S. Selected spot and marked it down.	
"	24		To PERONNE to see A.D.V.S. 5th Cavalry Division re mutual work of M.V.S. Fixed up and reported by 'phone to D.D.V.S. in evening. To FLAUCOURT, BARLEUX, VILLERS CARBONNEL and CHAPELLETTE, on reconnaissance with D.A.A. & Q.M.G. - Capt. Price-Jones and Gaunt called.	
"	25		Divisional H.Q. moved to PERONNE.	
"	26		My office moved to PERONNE	
"	27		I moved to PERONNE and cast round fixing up.	
"	28		Jones A.D.V.S. 5th Cavalry Division —	
"	29		Wired Leclair to move to HALLE. Capt Gaunt called in afternoon.	
"	30		Capt Bailey called. To DOINGT and TINCOURT to see H.Q. of 144th & 145th Bde. Brigades. Examined 5 captured enemy horses and arranges for their disposal to M.V.S. For mallein test. Saw Capt Price-Jones at TINCOURT.	
"	31		Divisional H.Q. moved to TINCOURT.	

CBM Harris M.C.
A.D.V.S. 48th Division

3/4/17

WAR DIARY or INTELLIGENCE SUMMARY

Army Form C. 2118.

ADVS 48
VETERINARY
48th (S.M.) DIVISION
Vol 25

Place	Date	Hour	Summary of Events and Information	Remarks and references to Appendices
H.Q. 48th Division	1917 April 1	5⁰	Office moved to BOIS de QUINCONCE.	
"	" 2		To HALLE to see M.V. Section. BDVS Fourth Army called. Round horses of M.M. Police	
"	" 3		Completed War Diary for March. To CHAPELLETTE to see horses of 5th Bn R Sussex Regt.	
"	" 4		Heavy snow fall. Office routine.	
"	" 5		To TINCOURT to see H.Q. horses. To H.Q. 4th Army. To Nivelle ao ADVS in a few days.	
"	" 9		To VILLERS BRETONNEUX to see ADVS 5th Cavalry Division.	
"	" 10		To VAUX to lecture to Fourth Army Artillery School.	
"	" 11		To FOUILLOY to see horses of 298 Bde R.F.A. 59 Division. To BAYON VILLERS with BSR Fault.	
"	" 12		Army to see horses of "N" Batty R.H.A. 5th Cavalry Division. Returned to Div H.A. To see CRA. To Conference of B.T.O's. Inf Bdes. at Head of A.A. & A.Reg. Put up suggestion to strengthen the position of B.T.O's. Approved and ordered.	
"	" 13		Round all horses of 48th Divisional Artillery with C.O's. & Capt Pinto Jones our Green. A.V.C.	
"	" 14		To BUIRE to reconnoitre a spot for an advanced M.V.S. Round horses of 7th & 8th Bn Worcestershire Regt.	
"	" 15		To LONGAVESNES, ST EMILIE, VILLERS FAUCON and TINCOURT WOOD to see all horses of 144 & 145 Inf Brigades. To see Brigadier commanding 144th Inf Brigade to report on the condition of his horse. B.T.O's accompanied me.	

Army Form C. 2118.

WAR DIARY
or
INTELLIGENCE SUMMARY.
(Erase heading not required.)

Instructions regarding War Diaries and Intelligence Summaries are contained in F.S. Regs., Part II. and the Staff Manual respectively. Title pages will be prepared in manuscript.

Place	Date	Hour	Summary of Events and Information	Remarks and references to Appendices
HQ 48 Division	April 15		Round horses of 48th Div. Signal Co. with Officer Commanding.	
"	16		To Adv. Mobile Vety. Section at BUIRE — Round debility horses of 241st Bde. R.F.A.	
"			To see mules of 1 Section of 48th D.A.C. Wired O.C. M.V.S. to move to BUIRE.	
"	17		Capt. Farrell ans returned to duty to-day. Barr of 7"B" Worcester Reg. went up. Killing of HQ & 2 D.D.'s ans made. Stephens to S.O.R. tonight. Army asking him to be sent. Busy half 8 animals to the Battalion which was consulted without him being agreed — Arrangements made to fetch these animals by 1/9 M.V.S.	
"	18		To HALLE to see M.V.S. Round debility horses of 241st Brigade R.F.A.	
"	19		Attended inspection by G.O.C. of horses of 48th Arkle. From Round horses of 143 Infantry Brigade at VILLERS FAUCON and SAULCOURT. Fell sick.	
April	20 Det S		Sick in tent.	
"	25		My Office moved to K.11.a.7.9. — Round HQ horses, MMP horses, and horses of 8th Bn. Worcestershire Regt.	
"	27		Conference of V.O's. Arranged work in new area.	
"	28		Round horses of 6 Gloster, 145 Ord. Bde. 145. M.G.C. 144 M.G.C. 145 M.S.C. 144 M.G.C. & 8th B. R. Warwick Regt. all a.m. rainy.	
"	29		To Div. Vy. horses of Corps Cavalry Squadron D.L.O. Germany	
"	30		To see M.V.S. at BUIRE.	

C. R. M. Farrel Lt. Col.
A.D. of V.S. 48th (S.M.) Division.
1/5/17.

Army Form C. 2118.

WAR DIARY
or
INTELLIGENCE SUMMARY.

VETERINARY 48th Division

Place	Date	Hour	Summary of Events and Information	Remarks and references to Appendices
Hd Qrs 48th Division	1917 May 1.		Ordered Capt. Farrell ave to remain in charge of mobile left on the line on Division moving back. Arranged with O/c 5th Bn R. Sussex Regt that Capt. Farrell billetted with them.	
"	2.		Capt. Farrell and Capt. Macconochie AVC called. To see horses of 5th R. Sussex Regt. CRA and staff left for TINCOURT.	
"	3.		1st (S.M) Mobile Vety. Section moved to HALLE on relief by (9th M.V.S, 42nd Division Hd. Qrs Division moved to FREMICOURT (PERONNE) to conform at D.D.V.S. Fourth Army Headquarters.	
"	4.		To M.V.S and fixed up transfer of surplus horses on return to UK. Br R. Warwickshire Regt To MESNIL to look horses of Bucks Battalion.	
"	5.		To CAPPY in morning. To BUIRE in evening to see 48 Divl. Train.	
"	6.		To see horses of 6th Bn. R. Warwickshire Regt, PERONNE and 143rd Machine Gun Co. To MP & Signal Co. in evening.	

WAR DIARY
or
INTELLIGENCE SUMMARY.
(Erase heading not required.)

Army Form C. 2118.

Place	Date	Hour	Summary of Events and Information	Remarks and references to Appendices
H.Q. 48th Division	May 7.		DDVS Fourth Army called. He sanctioned 10 days ordinary leave for Capt. V. Pryce Jones A.V.C.	
"	8.		Capt. Pryce Jones left on 16 days leave. Round H.Q. and Signal Co. horses.	
"	9.		Round horses of 143rd Infantry Brigade with B.T.O. and T.O's. To M.V.S. at HALLE — Capt Green called.	
"	10.		To H.Q. 2nd Corps at CATELET and CARTIGNY, to observe working of Corps mobile Veterinary detachment.	
"	11.		Round H.Q. horses. Capt. Gaunt, Dakrey Green called. To M.V.S. at HALLE with DDR Fourth Army, who inspected I.8 pack horses, surplus to division.	
"	12.		Ordered 1 N.C.O and 3 men of 1st S.M. M.V.S. now with 3rd Corps M.V. Detachment, to be returned to their unit, as division is leaving the Corps. To see DDVS Fourth Army. To see area to locate site	

Army Form C. 2118.

WAR DIARY
or
INTELLIGENCE SUMMARY.
(Erase heading not required.)

Instructions regarding War Diaries and Intelligence Summaries are contained in F. S. Regs., Part II. and the Staff Manual respectively. Title pages will be prepared in manuscript.

Place	Date	Hour	Summary of Events and Information	Remarks and references to Appendices
HQ 3 48th Division	May 12		To M.V.S. Forest II Division M.V.S. proposing its establishment to M.V.S. of 3rd Anzac Division. On return reported this fact to D.D.V.S. Fifth Army, who promised to rectify.	
"	13		Wire received from D.D.V.S. Fifth Army confirming his admin of powers conveying that day Division in Fifth Army - there take over the site of 11th Division M.V.S. Capt. Gant called - Ordered his move to BEAULENCOURT M.V.S. D.D.V.S. Fourth Army to arrange charge of III Corps Heavy artillery units, early in one of Capt. Green a/c acting for Capt. Machonie on leave.	
"	14		M.V.S. moved to new area at N.17.6.	
"	15		Ordered Capt. Farrell to rejoin 48th D.A.C. We come under orders of Fifth Army to day.	
"	16		Division H.Q. moved to N.11 Central. To see M.V.S. To VELU to see site for Divisional Advanced HQ & Saw Signal Co. lines.	

A 5834 Wt. W 4973/M 687 750,000 8/16 D. D. & L. Ltd. Forms/C.2118/13.

Army Form C. 2118.

WAR DIARY
or
INTELLIGENCE SUMMARY.
(Erase heading not required.)

IV

Place	Date	Hour	Summary of Events and Information	Remarks and references to Appendices
H.Q. 48th Division	May 15		To see H.Q. horses of R.E.	
	16		To H.Q. horses and M.V.S.	
	17		Round horses of 3rd Field Ambulance. Round H.Q. horses. Round horses of 48 Divisional Train at FREMICOURT.	
	18		Round H.Q. horses, and H.Qrs Signal horses — Capt Green to swing club	
	19		Orders received to take on duties of D.D.V.S. Fifth Army, vice Col. Lena Coyngham reported sick — To HQ'rs Fifth Army.	
	20		Capt. G.H. Farrell of A.D.V.S. 48th Division. I regret being my failing to	
	15		direct him, he has kept no diary	
	31st			
	4 June 1917			

C.S.M. Hearns Lt Col.
A.D.V.S. 48th Division.

WAR DIARY or INTELLIGENCE SUMMARY

Army Form C. 2118.

VETERINARY
48th Division Vol I 27

Place	Date	Hour	Summary of Events and Information	Remarks and references to Appendices
HQ 48th Div	1917 June 1 to 5		Capt. Y.H. Farrell, A.D.V.S. - No diary kept, not having been instructed to keep one -	
	June 6		Lt. Col. C.B.M. Harris P.S.O. rejoined Division from Fifth Army and resumed duties as A.D.V.S.	
	7		Round H.Q. horses - To HAPLINCOURT & BAPAUME locating units of Division	
	8		To HAPLIN COURT, DELSAUX FARM, & VILLERS AU FLOS. Conference all V.O's present but Capt Y.H. Farrell - Round horses of 240 Bde R.F.A. with V.O. Y.C.	
	9		To 48 Div Train - In H.Q. 48 D.A.C.	
	10		Round all units of 48 D.A.C. with Y.C. & V.O. Y.C. In C.O.'s Conference	
	11		Lt Col C.B.M. Harris P.S.O. left on 10 days leave. Capt Y.H. Farrell A.V.C. took over charge with all V.O.'s to lecture by Div Gas Officer on Anti-Gas Horse Respirator.	
	12			
	13		Routine	
	14		Routine - To D.D.V.S. office ALBERT.	
	15		Routine - To 48 Div Train	
	16		Routine - Judging P.H.Q. Horse Show	
	17		Inspected No 8 Gd. Found everything quite satisfactory. Inspected Transport horses of 144 Inf. Bde.	

Army Form C. 2118.

WAR DIARY
or
INTELLIGENCE SUMMARY.
(Erase heading not required.)

Place	Date	Hour	Summary of Events and Information	Remarks and references to Appendices
H.Q 48th Div	June 19		Routine	
"	20		At the request of Lt. Col. Barrett M.A. & R.M.C. inspected all animals of Units in HAPLINCOURT in conjunction with V.O. to Australian Units in the village of Nrange. Found 9 cases of Mange in 50th Battery 13th Brigade 5th Australian Division. All other units in HAPLINCOURT were inspected by me and found free from Mange. Inspected horses of 5th Br. R. Sussex R.	
"	21		Inspected 143 Inf Bde horses. Transferred 2 Surplus riders from M.V.S. to 8th R. War R.	
"	22		Routine	
"	23		Lt. Col. C.B.M. Harris P.S.O. returned from leave. Received orders to join IV Corps. — Round H.Q. horses.	
"	24		Lt. Col. C.B.M. Harris P.S.O. left 48th Division and joined IV Corps.	
"	25		Major A.H. Rea A.V.C. Joined A.D. Dir. & assumes duties of DADVS Inspected m.t & c horses of 1 2 3 & Coys Div Train	
"	26		Incl 110 Remounts at ACHIET-LE-GRAND. 50 L.D. for Div Arty, 5th C. 19 R. 5 LD & 31 HD for other units. Approxer, dishibited also other 60 fr other units	

WAR DIARY
or
INTELLIGENCE SUMMARY.
(Erase heading not required.)

Army Form C. 2118.

Place	Date	Hour	Summary of Events and Information	Remarks and references to Appendices
H.Q. 48th	June 27		Visited lorries D.H.Q. M.M.P. 10 Coveries C.R.E. Capt Farrell returned to duty with D.A.C.	
	28		Office. Attended C.O.'s conference	
	29		Visited 144, 145, 190 transport. M.V.S. 3rd F.A.	
	30		Visited D.H.Q. 144, 145, 190 transport	

30 June 1917

Aus. Reg. Maj.
D.A.D.V.S. 48th Div.

WAR DIARY or INTELLIGENCE SUMMARY

Army Form C. 2118.

D.A.D.V.S.
48TH (S.M.) DIVISION.
V.S. 1/32
Date: 28/7/17

Place	Date	Hour	Summary of Events and Information	Remarks and references to Appendices
BEAULENCOURT P de C.	July 1st 1917		Routine:	
	2		Routine: 4 cases received:	
	3		Six cases evacuated to 49 Vety Hosp: DADVS called: section moved to BIHUCOURT (P de C)	
BIHUCOURT P d C ADINFER	4		Section moved to ADINFER (P d C)	
	5		Routine: DADVS called.	
	6		Routine: one case received: TT02168 Cpl Larrau sent on leave.	
	7		Routine: four cases received: TT02163 Sgr W. Bray appointed P/A/S/Sgt Secy as from 3/7/17.	
	8		Routine: two cases received: TT02185 Pte Burke & TT02220 Pte Bs sent to VII Corps range Dept (MONDICOURT) DADVS called.	
	9		Routine: one case received: TT02363 P/A/S/Sgt Secy, T/F/298393 Pte Orme, TT02940 Pte Burn, TT02114 Pte Burke	
	10		Routine: four cases received: eight cases evacuated to No 9 Vety Hosp: returned leave.	
	11		Routine: one case received: DADVS called: G.O.C. 48 Div inspected section.	
	12		Routine: five cases received:	
	13		Routine: one case received: DADVS called.	
	14		Routine:	
	15		Routine:	

J. E. Gauntt
Capt/AVC

Army Form C. 2118.

WAR DIARY
or
INTELLIGENCE SUMMARY.
(Erase heading not required.)

Instructions regarding War Diaries and Intelligence Summaries are contained in F. S. Regs., Part II. and the Staff Manual respectively. Title pages will be prepared in manuscript.

Place	Date	Hour	Summary of Events and Information	Remarks and references to Appendices
ADINFER P.d.C	1917 July 16		Routine:	
"	17		Routine: Two cases received.	
"	18		Routine: five cases received.	
"	19		Routine: two cases received: D.A.D.V.S. called: hoSE21MSPL-Pervis joined for duty from No 1 F.H.	
"	20		Routine: one case received	
"	21		Eleven cases evacuated to ThoyRly Hospl. Section entrained at Mondicourt at 8 p.m. (P.d.C)	
"	22		Section detrained at GODVAERSVELDE at 6am. and marched to VOGELTJE P.d.C. ADVS 18 "Corps called.	
"	23		Routine: T4/248393 Dr Dunn returned from leave	
"	24		Routine:	
"	25		Routine: TT02163 P/A/S/Sgt Ray, TT02170 Pt Brown, T7625 by Pt Lock returned from leave. TT02172 Pt Vickers A.W. re'ton leave	
"	26		Section moved to HAMHOEK - F30A64 (SheT27): four cases received: D.A.D.V.S called	
"	27		Routine: hofy four SE 9673 Pt Coghlin F.W. joined for duty from No 2 F.H.	
"	28		" : one case received: Thirty four cases evacuated to XVIII Corps M.C.D.	
"	29		" : seven cases received: five cases evacuated to XVIII Corps M.D.	
"	30		" : five cases received: five cases evacuated to XVIII Corps M.V.D: DADVS called	
"	31		" : one case received E Grand Capt A.V.C. 4th S.M., M.V.S

Army Form C. 2118.

WAR DIARY
or
INTELLIGENCE SUMMARY.
(Erase heading not required.)

VETERINARY DIVISIONAL Vol 29

Place	Date	Hour	Summary of Events and Information	Remarks and references to Appendices
Hd. 2nd 48th Div. 18th Corps area	1917 Aug 1		Official. Inspected lines 3rd Fd Amb c	ansr
	2		Inspected lines 1st Fd Amb c - 143 Inf. Bde. Visited M.V.S. - relieved 39th Divn Advanced & Receiving DMV and Farm	ansr
	3		Conference of V.Os.	ansr
	4		Advanced compare at A.D.V.S 18 Corps. Visited M.V.S. 1st Fd Ambc	ansr
	5		Visited D.A.C 240, 241 R.F.A. A.V.D.Sn	ansr
	6		Visited A.V.D.Sn. 3rd Fd Amb M.V.S.	ansr
	7		Move office to C camp. Sent in change of postponing emb from 39th Divn - 134, 182, 135, R.F.A, 35th D.A.C. 1 Coy Train, 13th Divn & later Rgl 234, 225, 227 Fd Coy R.E. 155 Army Troops, 150, 34 m.c. Visited 1st Fd Amb. M.V.S. 7th Wwomen. 13th Bn GloRs.	ansr
	8		Inspected lines 143 Inf. Bde. 234, 225, 227 Fd Co R.E. Lys area.	ansr
	9		Visited 7th Wwomen. 1, 2, 3 Co Fd Amb c M.V.S	ansr
	10		Conference of V.Os. Examined 12 subaltern riders at one Train transferred to H.S.H. and remounts at Baron - 50 L.D.M, 36 L.D.M = Septr sick ans 4 L.D. 20 M.D. 1 P 5.25 fr oth anx. Total 109	ansr

Army Form C. 2118.

WAR DIARY
or
INTELLIGENCE SUMMARY.

VETERINARY

(Erase heading not required.)

Instructions regarding War Diaries and Intelligence Summaries are contained in F.S. Regs., Part II. and the Staff Manual respectively. Title pages will be prepared in manuscript.

Place	Date	Hour	Summary of Events and Information	Remarks and references to Appendices
	Aug 11		Attend conference at A.D.V.S. 18 Corps	Appx
	12		Inspected at lines of 143 Sup. Coy. Visited 3rd Fd Amb. C.R.E.	Appx
	13		Visited 1st & 2nd Fd Amb. Afternoon. Visited 1, 2, 3 Fd Amb. remounts horses/or remounts & 145 Sup. Coy.	Appx
	14		Visited 3rd Army HQr R.F.A. and Fd. Army's horses & mess	Appx
	15		Visited Sig. Coy. R.E. 1, 2 & 3 Cos. Fd Amb.	Appx
	16		Visited 143 Sup. Coy. Signals Coy. M.V.S.	Appx
	17		Conference of V.Os. Inspected horses of 24, 13m R.F.A.	Appx
	18		Attended conference at A.D.V.S. Inspected horses of 24 13m 15 F.A. with Supt Veter	Appx
	19		Visited Sig. Co. 143 Sup. Co. 3m 141 Labour Coy. M.E.D.	Appx
	20		Inspected 24.0. 24, 13m R.F.A. with A.D.V.S.	Appx
	21		Visited A.V.C. the remount at Croix - Lutulede came to Div Army 15 C.D.M. 10.2.0m. Also visits 38 C.D.M. 37 M.D. Lund. Coy	Appx
	22		Visited 141 Lab. Co. Sig. & R.E. M.V.D.	Appx
	23		Visited 3rd Army HQ Ady 13m, 14m g Sup. R.G. Sig. G. Divny meet at lunch 9-30 am left my administration & lunch 9 23 when arrival (R.F.A. R.E. H.C. 190 G.R.S.C.)	Appx

WAR DIARY
or
INTELLIGENCE SUMMARY.

VETERINARY III

Army Form C. 2118.

Place	Date	Hour	Summary of Events and Information	Remarks and references to Appendices
	Augt	24	Conference of V.Os. Visited 103/Bde R.F.A.	AvR
		25	Arranged conference of A.D.V.S. Visited 25th D.A.C.	AvR
		26	Visited M.E.S arrangements re horsing Cadre of A.V.C. Works Coy. B.	AvR
		27	Visited M.V.S. Movements at Proven. Div Arty L.D.H.100. Units L.Dm 45	AvR
		28	Visited M.V.S. A.D.S. Movements at Proven. L.Km. 31. Handed over advance Units to 5=5th Bde. Moved office to workout.	AvR
Workout		29	Office. Visited DS4 2.6 Sig. Cos horses	AvR
"		30	Visited 143. 144. 145 Inf. Bdes. 4.5 Bde. Trans 42. 8th D.A	AvR
"		31	Visited M.M.P. + 58" Bath 34" A.d.A.B.	AvR

AvR.d

WAR DIARY
or
INTELLIGENCE SUMMARY.
(Erase heading not required.)

Army Form C. 2118.

D.A.D.V.S.
48TH
(S.M.) DIVISION.
No. V.S. 163

DADVS 48
VETERINARY I

Place	Date	Hour	Summary of Events and Information	Remarks and references to Appendices
WORMHOUT	Sept 1		Attended conference at A.D.V.S. Visited M.V.S.	AwR
"	2		Inspection lorries 52 Bn 34 A.H.Bns.	AwR
"	3		Visited Sup. Bn. M.V.S.	AwR
"	4		Visited 143, 144 Insp Bns & motors surplus animal	AwR
"	5		Office. Visited Hq Co. R.E. 1st/2nd M.M.P.	AwR
"	6		Visited M.V.S. 57 Bn Dm 34 A.H.Bn. Capt Grant went on 10 days leave	AwR
"	7		Visited D.G.R.C. DH 2	AwR
"	8		Attended conference at A.D.V.S.	AwR
"	9		Visited M.V.S.	AwR
"	10		Insp. Reid meat not needed Removed to 13th C.C.S.	
"	11		Capt Ride Jones recommended of DADVS.	
"	12		Moved Office to St Jan-ter-Biezen. Visited F.S.A.13 Inspecting of Brit H.D. horses + Brit Ripes Isst M.V.S.	
"	13		Capt Darley prest with accident	
"	14		Inspected sick Case of Britain 1st Inf. Bn. 1/2 Herts Welshm 7/45 Inf Bde	
"	15		Capt Lane took over Duties (AVC) 11-9-17. Capt Darley Sent to Hospital	
"	16		Attended A.D.V.S. Conference. Visit M.V.S. and Inspected animals for wounds.	
"	17		En Loute of travel to ZUTKERQUE.	

WAR DIARY or INTELLIGENCE SUMMARY

Army Form C. 2118.

VETERINARY

Place	Date	Hour	Summary of Events and Information	Remarks and references to Appendices
LONGPRÉ	18.9.17	Tues.	Reported for duty as ADVS to 48th Division. Called on DADVS & ADMS. Withdrew tup. Instructed Capt. Ride-Jones to inspect mules & meat escort at AUDRICQ.	NS
"	19th	Wed.	Called on A.P.M. A.D.V.S. acted as Railway Interpreter. Saw H.Q. Envir./A S.M. Field Ambulance. Food working Oatmeal hrs 1/4.5 Coy. Ba. Returned mmn. from Pailleul for 2 hrs Lus 1/4.5 M.G. Coy. Animals in very poor shape for night's work and 1st Nfd. 2nd Donsets 2.0 Satisfactory. Visit 8th Manchester. Lord Derby's battn. not fed 5 manner.	NS
"	20th	Thurs.	Visits to H.Q. 1/4 5th Bn. Signals, (Fanny Poor). Visit 1/6 Bn. Recollanes. Attached to A.D.V. Samples of 1/5 Bn. & Amb. & Gpt. Gmitter asked attention. Feed 1/3 Gv. Field Ambulance. Invited feed. Attended 186 horses out of Stables. Inspected M.M.P. Brow.	NS
"	21st	Fri.	Visit to no 3 Remount Depot. Orders and over 20 Riders.	NS
"	22nd	Sat.	Distributed 20 Riders. Invited Inspected hy 3 Gv & 1/4.5 Brig. All out. parking Hy M.P. Capt. J. Saunders A.V.C. reported to me for duty.	NS
"	23rd	Sun.	Visit 1/4.5 M.G. Sec. Evacuated up for debility. Visit 1/3 Field Ambulance.	NS
"	24th	Mon.	Employing lands as to fitting for the Road, H.Q. Am. Subsistence 1/ Manchester. No 2 & 1/4 Glam. Coy. 8 Manchester. gst manners. transport WR. Batn. 1/1 RFA Oxford & Bucks. 1st manners. Capt. Ride-Jones Genl. St Manny attach. starting 14/9/17 R.F. Bde from O.H.(S.E.) from 240 Bde R.F.A. 6.4.8. med turn. vice Capt. A.G. Dowling MM. Evacuated sick 15/9/17. Patient. Captd. bomb A.V.P. (Y.C.) joined hirer 23/9/17 and to get put for duty. He was Bon. RFA from 24/9/17.	NS
"	25th	Tues.	Visits H.Q. 1/5 Warwicks. No 3 Coy. Train.	NS

Army Form C. 2118.

WAR DIARY
or
INTELLIGENCE SUMMARY.

~~VETERINARY~~

(Erase heading not required.)

Place	Date	Hour	Summary of Events and Information	Remarks and references to Appendices
ZUTKERKE	1	6pm	Visit H.Q. Visit 58th Manchester. Visit No 1 S/S Mobilaire. Sent up from ?	N.B.
"	2	9am	Horses on to new position.	N.B.
"	"	"	Visit No 2 8th Worcester. To 3 Cav. Brn.	N.B.
Front Camp	9	8am Sunday	Loan Office to 76 & 28 Skeits. Enrolled at 82nd M.S. and his Cavl. Guard. Visit to M.V.S. + office, 1st Coy B.	N.B.
"	29	10½	Attended Conference of A.D.S. & DAQMG. [?] re Buglehooks call at office/DDS S/Camp. Inspected 4 & 8 Coys M.V.S. and 58 Brit M.V.S. Instructed letter, + set on on men to carry Remounts. Lantern 1 in conducting N.C.O. Capts Taylor, Richards and Heath. Kgy L St ?? to load to refront. Capt. Grant called to consult about a Brit. hoofed case	N.B.
"	30	noon	? to 290 Bde R.F.A. and Inspected "A" and "B" Btys Horses. ? going round approx. Cont. 12 Jas. Saturday Senior ? sick R. Officer or Staff Officer Inspection. Rides + evening to 48 Brit M.V.S.	N.B.

W. Stockwell. Maj.
ADVS "8 Corps"

WAR DIARY or INTELLIGENCE SUMMARY

Army Form C. 2118

DADVS 2
VETERINARY J
V.S. 17 31

Place	Date	Hour	Summary of Events and Information	Remarks and references to Appendices
"C" Corps Nr POPERINGHE.	Sept 1		Visit 8th Mounteds. (good) Visit 444 F. Ho. Cy R.E. (good). Visit 4/44 2nd Cy R.E.c	
			Visit "16 R. Warwicks. Visit Scar. Pierres. Y good. Visit A Sqdn N.Z.H.	
			Visit and inspected all animals.	
	2		Inspected all animals of 291 Bole. A75 C+D. Found/case Mange	
			Visits to 48th Div M.V.S. and 58th Div M.V.S. Animals and Staff management excellent	
			Had Orderroom on 2 Cases with 37 S. 5th Army Re. Chief Packing N.Z.H.	
			Visits D.D. Div Signals. 1st Anzac. Re. arranged V. O'book.	
	3		Visits H.Q. Div Signals. 8th Div. Amm. Sub. 58th Div M.V.S.	
	4		Visit 58th Div M.V.S.	
	5		Held Conference at my Office. Present. O/C Corps Trps R.E Col Crawshaw General, Veglao Rushmere & Sheather	
			Visits to 1/3 Yo. Ambulance. Trps R.E + at Office. & Div M.V.S. Visited in pat H.q. Signals.	
	6		Attended Conference A.D.S 18th Corps. Visits Div. Vet. Posts. both Divl M.V.S.	
			477 40 Cy R.E. and 7th Sussex. Cap Gaunt called.	
	7		Visits to both M.V.S.O. Visit Div Train and Inspected 92 Bumped Cases Accompanied	
			by Capt Ridr. Jones, ho measures with S.A. dogs to be taken. Visits 6th + 9th Warwicks	
			143 Bar M.C Gun. Trps of N.Z.E.H. at Canal Bank. 1/2 Yo. Ambulance	
	8		Visits to 6th 2nd M.V.S. and 58th Div M.V.S	

WAR DIARY or INTELLIGENCE SUMMARY.

Army Form C. 2118.

11

Place	Date	Hour	Summary of Events and Information	Remarks and references to Appendices
"C" Corps N. POPERINGHE	9/17		Visit 48th Bn. M.V.S. and Promulgated F.P.M. Sentence on Pte Taggart A.V.C.	
			Visit 58th Bn. M.V.S. Visit Units at Canal Bank. Severed Office & Albert Shed 28	
			Handed over 58th Div. duty and 2/ End M.V.S. to 84 B.V.S. 9th Divn.	
"X" Corps — do	10		Visit 48th Bn. M.V.S. Visit H.2 1st B.Bn. arranged for Pte Taggart's Sentence	
			to be carried out 11/9 to 5th Dragoon Regt.	
	11		Visit M.V.S. Gave of Orders re repeats. Use of Anti-Tetanic Serum & Red round Cards	
			Inspected 3 Coys Div Train. Visited Div Signals T.H.2.	
	12		Visit M.V.S. H.2. Signals. Prepared Hockey returns.	
PERNES	13		Moved Office from 1st Corps Area, to PERNES, 5th Corps Area	
"	14		No Div's Horse transport in Area.	
	15		Vet Dir M.V.S. at Unknowing Station Arranged 2nd Canadian M.V.S. to receive	
			46th Div. M.V.S. until Me exchange at the 17 A.H. 31 locator. ACCS Shed 5.1.8.	
			Capt Frisk Jones called. Orders from Asst G report when from Cdn. Called at office.	
			of A.D.V.S. 5th Corps.	
	16		Visit Dir M.V.S. & H.2.	
VILLERS CHATEL	17		Moved Office from PERNES to VILLERS CHATEL	

WAR DIARY or INTELLIGENCE SUMMARY

Army Form C. 2118.

VETERINARY

III

Place	Date	Hour	Summary of Events and Information	Remarks and references to Appendices
West 13 (36B)	Oct 18		Moved offices from TILLERS GRATES to Chateau d'Acq at W30.b.53. Shel 36B.	
			Visit A.D.V.S. reference Vety Supervision of Rest Billets. Issue of H.R. Horse Lines.	
			Visit 4 & 5 Coy R.E. Visit Div M.V.S.	
	19		Visit 6th Workers Lame debility Cases. Visit 8th Workers (good). Visit M.S. Visit 1st Workers (g) Visit 44th A.A Coy R.E. (good) Visit 24th Ay P.A (Inf B.)	
	20		Visit A.D.V.S. Conference. Visit 1/3 Fd Ambulance	
	21		Visit Div. Tran. Redistributed 11 Officers. Issue of H.Ms.Bn. 2 Coy Trans for Use. Visit M.Y.S.	
	22		Visit 1 AM Lorries 2nd Ambulance. 4th Workers. 6th Workers. 40 of 14/5 Bde. 5 Workers.	
			L.O.C. & Bn. and Div M.Y.S.	
	23		Transferred / Gun from A.P.M. to F. Ridley R.P. Visit Fd Ambulance & transferred	
			1 H.D. 6 1/3 Fd Ambulance. Visit 1/3 Fd Amb.	
	24		7:30 am Col. Mapwells Charger. Visit with Staff Capt. to 240th Bde R.F.A & inspected the	
			4 B.C.s Picked animals to Remain for Debility as follows, from "B" 51, "C" 15,	
			"A" 9, "B" 12. Suggested Charge of 9th May 6 "B" Bty, the animals of this Bty.	
			being an all round neglected lot, with many hard off pulled A.C.V.D. "poor"	
	25		Wrote O.C.A.V.C advising Maker Stophe for Div M.V.S & Brit M.V.S. H.2, Visit Div team	

WAR DIARY or INTELLIGENCE SUMMARY

Army Form C. 2118

VETERINARY — IV

Place	Date	Hour	Summary of Events and Information	Remarks and references to Appendices
N30/5/3 (36A) Oct	25	Morn.	Inspected all numbers of 241 Bde. RFA. Picks walks following for Evacuation to Schilto. "A" 24, 13. "B" 14. "C" 14. 9/14. the horses of "A" "B" & "C" Btys. are generally speaking in fair condition considering their recent conditions of work. "D" Bty are "poor" all round.	
	26		Inspected H.Q. and all R.A.C. excepting M/S. M.T. "A" Echelon very satisfactory. Zero poor "condition" but not requiring evacuation. Visit to M.T.S.	
	27		Attended A.D.V.S. conference. Inspected to/Sec. "A" Echelon D.A.C. Return. Visit to plan Bombs, watch. Visit to 7th Rant. A.R.M. Minor 15 Horses, + M/S. D.V.S. Called at my Office re. Cox of Ebryonic lymphongites in R/Co. A/Sec. Examined D.D.V.S. and M.D.S. to the M.V.S. and our team. investigating Case of L. lymphangites. Expected & inspected. Made report for D.V.S. Conference with all my F.O.'s etc.	
	29		Capt. Vardi-Jones started 14 days General leave. Instructed Col. Pere to do work of own. Saw army horses at source. Visit unit of 145 Dy. Bde. Visit of Inspection alone with Col. Pere NR. 240 Bde. RFA. Interview that Command Forms Emplacement.	

www.ingramcontent.com/pod-product-compliance
Lightning Source LLC
Chambersburg PA
CBHW081552160426
43191CB00011B/1907